PRAYERS AND MEDITATIONS

PRAYERS AND MEDITATIONS

Edited by GERALD HEARD

Wipf & Stock
PUBLISHERS
Eugene, Oregon

Wipf and Stock Publishers
199 W 8th Ave, Suite 3
Eugene, OR 97401
www.wipfandstock.com

Prayers and Meditations
Selections by Gerald Heard, Aldous Huxley, and Others
Edited by Gerald Heard

ISBN 13: 978-1-55635-096-2
ISBN 10: 1-55635-096-1

Publication date: 1/1/2008
Previously published by Harper & Brothers, 1949

Photograph of Gerald Heard by Jay Michael Barrie

Acknowledgments:
The Barrie Family Trust gratefully acknowledges the following permissions: "Comments on Prayers and Meditations" by Marvin Barrett reprinted by permission of The Estate of Marvin Barrett. "Seven Meditations" by Aldous Huxley reprinted by permission of Laura Huxley. The meditation on "Mortification" reprinted by permission of William H. Forthman, PhD. The meditation on "Purity" reprinted by permission of William H. Forthman, PhD, assignee to the publications rights of Margaret Gage.

Series Foreword

Gerald Heard (Oct. 6, 1889–Aug. 14, 1971) wrote nearly forty books during the course of a distinguished career. His Cambridge-trained, curiosity-ridden mind left no stone unturned in its intellectual investigations. His nonfiction topics ranged from history to philosophy, from psychology to religion, and virtually everything in between. These issues were woven together by a single unifying theme—the evolution of consciousness. During the 1940s, after he had relocated to America, after he had rediscovered his religious roots, and after he had begun a rigorous daily meditation practice, Gerald, as he was always known, mobilized his energies into establishing Trabuco College in Southern California. Trabuco was the first coeducational spiritual community in America to incorporate ecumenical, nonsectarian religious principles and practices. And practice the Trabuco attendees did, meditating three times daily in order to accelerate the spiritual evolution of their own individual consciousnesses.

Having previously published a dozen mostly academic and popular science books, Gerald turned his attention to religion during this war-torn decade. Gerald's religious writings from this period consist of eight key contributions that address practical and inspirational spiritual themes. Of these, four primary Heardian religious works are initially included in this vital new Wipf & Stock series, with more to follow. Collectively these books comprise Gerald's quintessential statements on the spiritual path, and a person could conceivably use these volumes as guidebooks for their entire spiritual journey.

And here is Gerald at his very best—preaching the evolution of consciousness and offering practical advice on how to attain it. Gerald's rotating roles as visionary historian, maverick cosmologist, and prescient philosopher are all present in the background of these religious works. But at the forefront is Gerald the practicing mystic and knowing docent, gushing forth an ebullient but sometimes cautionary narrative on traversing the spiritual path from start to finish. His accounts, as confirmed by classic mystics and traditional texts, derive from his own subjective experience. The ringing truth of his musings will cause the receptive reader first to reflect, then to act, propelled by the stirring contagion of Gerald's boundless enthusiasm.

In the 1940s, novelist Christopher Isherwood wrote that Gerald, "has influenced the thought of our time, directly and indirectly, to an extent which will hardly be appreciated for another fifty years." Those fifty years have now passed. Some of Gerald's ideas have fallen by the wayside, while others lie dormant still waiting to sprout. Yet a good many have blossomed into unspoken cornerstones of contemporary thought. The widespread establishment of religious communities has become commonplace. Religious syncretism, ecumenical studies, and interdisciplinary, eclectic approaches lie at the vanguard of progressive religious thought. Contemplative meditation practices have gained broad acceptance across a spectrum of diverse traditions. Theories on the evolution of consciousness abound. Colleges and whole movements of thought now regularly explore the transpersonal realm of pure consciousness.

But what makes Gerald's farsighted approach to religion especially relevant now is what made it relevant when these books were first published—he is espousing timeless truths. The reader is supplied with a map, compass, and numerous exhortations of attainment, as well as warnings of the pitfalls to avoid while embarking on this singlemost important sojourn in life. Gerald offered no quick fixes or shortcuts. He advocated a wholesale restructuring of one's entire being through, "the skilled, conscious training of our spirits." He advanced a holistic approach long before holistic approaches became popular.

Within these books is found Gerald's essential message: "Our whole life must become intentional and purposive, instead of a series of irrelevant events, adventures, and accidents. We must ourselves deliberately develop ourselves. That evolution which follows will show itself in a threefold development: in growth of conduct, of character and of consciousness itself. The world exists for man to achieve union with God. The meaning of all, the purpose and the end of all is one thing, seeing God."

When revisiting Gerald's spiritual classics in this new century, we are entering the very heart of religious experience. We are treading the path trodden by serious spiritual practitioners, be they novices or seasoned mystics. We are undertaking a journey of utmost significance, leading to pulsating union with God. As able guide and modern interpreter of mysticism, Gerald Heard nimbly and authoritatively beckons us toward the Goal that each of us was born to realize in this very life.

John Roger Barrie
Literary Executor of Gerald Heard
Nevada City, California
January 22, 2007

Thanks especially to Ted Lewis of Wipf and Stock Publishers, and Craig Tenney and Phyllis Westberg of Harold Ober Associates for their valuable assistance in bringing this series into print.

For more information on Gerald Heard, visit geraldheard.com, the Gerald Heard Official Website.

—JRB

Comments on Prayers and Meditations

by Marvin Barrett

New York City, October 2004

IN MAY 1942, just six months after the U.S. entry into World War II and a few days past my 22nd birthday, a mimeographed sheaf of seven of the meditations included in this small volume was pressed into my hand by Gerald Heard, its editor. I was a provisional ensign in the United States Naval Reserve, headed God knows where in a world where the bad guys seemed to be in charge and pressing their advantage.

It could have been considered strange under such circumstances to be given page-long considerations of Being, Beauty (I), Love, Grace (I), Holiness, Peace, and Joy;[1] less strange when one considered that I was embarking on a regimen of prayer and meditation that would carry me through the next rocky four years. And even less strange when one realized that these short elegant statements were written by Aldous Huxley, the man whose conversion from one of the era's prime cyn-

1. Editor's note: Under each of these chapters, Aldous Huxley's contributions consist of the Meditation section only.

ics to a true believer in the spiritual meaning of life had triggered my own, from cocky Harvard senior to goggle-eyed seeker after truth, the truth expounded with such informed conviction by Gerald Heard, the author of the majority of the selections that follow.

Even more remarkable was the fact that upon my rediscovery of this lode of spiritual aspirations forty years later they seemed as potent and apt as they had when I first made their acquaintance. A further explanation of these statements' effectiveness may lie in the fact that, as pointed out in the Introduction, the bulk of those not by Huxley, "can be read as a kind of impersonal autobiography" of their author, Gerald Heard, who wanted to remain anonymous. "They are the imprints left by an attempt at a group religious life." This refers to Trabuco College, an interfaith-religious commune that Heard founded in 1942 in the foothills of Southern California.

Involved in this experiment, which, alas, was dissolved shortly before *Prayers and Meditations* was published, were a distinguished group of writers and editors, laypersons and spiritual pilgrims. The list, headed by Heard and Huxley, included Christopher Isherwood, John Van Druten, Betsey Barton, Felix Greene, Franklin Kelley, Denver Lindley, Lucille Nixon, Allan and Elizabeth Hunter, Eugene Exman, Margaret Gage, William Forthman, and Michael Barrie. In my opinion, their talents and counsel were never better employed. And this present collection, which Heard refers to as, "a section of chart readings from the record of a voyage," ably and aptly epitomizes not only Gerald's lofty aspirations but also those of all of us who were for a time a part of the noble experiment that was Trabuco College.

* * * * * * *

Marvin Barrett (1920–2006) led an esteemed career as author of 14 books and editor of several noted magazines. For 16 years he served as senior lecturer at the Columbia University School of Journalism, and he was founding director of its prestigious Alfred I. DuPont Survey and Awards in Broadcast Journalism. After his retirement he was for many years a senior editor at *Parabola* magazine.

CONTENTS

INTRODUCTION

THESE prayers and meditations are traces of an experiment. They are imprints left by an attempt at a group religious life. As such they may yield hints to other seekers. For they grew out of a convergent effort of a number of people to help one another toward a common goal. Group worship gradually precipitates a pattern. Prayer practiced in common creates its own "score." These prayers and meditations evolved. There is nothing individual, original or literary about them. Seven were written by one of our ablest authors.[1] But, as much as the others, they were not composed as examples of style. Indeed style and significance are furthest apart in prayer. It will be obvious that they are all, more or less, reflections. That is to say, they are musings and desires (considerations and aspirations) shaped by the traditional recollections and prayers. They are present-day renderings of those thoughts and feelings which have been rising in men since they began to reach out to Him who is beyond the senses. These short passages are then echoes. But an echo can be more than an imitation. We hear harmonics when sound is given back from

[1] Mr. Aldous Huxley.

certain surfaces. Echo-sounding gives an accurate outline of the sea floor. Though then these brief phrases of worship are shaped from the traditional language to express a common experience, they may have some value for other seekers who share the same wish, who find that the constant set and current of their will to live intentionally, their constant desire to be aware of God, does gradually carve itself a channel of expression. The pages that follow can be read as a kind of impersonal autobiography, fragments from a logbook, a section of chart readings from the record of a voyage. The material grew for some six or seven years. Gradually it took shape, made itself into a pattern from daily use and that pattern tended to become a monthly cycle or rhythm. Weekly repetition was tried. But that tended to "wear the nap off" even the best prayer, psalm or passage. A quarterly cycle—though there is much to say for the ninety-day rhythm—proved somewhat too long for general purposes. For in that case the prayer or meditation, instead of becoming too familiar, had not enough repetition to grow sufficiently well-known. Indeed two things seem to be necessary if spoken prayer is to prove most helpful: The first is an optimum length. Long-winded prayer soon outruns the soul, ceases to be prayer. Fine phrase distracts. Even more disturbing is any drift toward argument. The deepest prayer, no doubt, is silent. But few can sustain that. We need, ever so often, brief reminders to send us back to our silent waiting. Words, like breakers on a beach, can carry us up the shore. But they will carry us out again if we don't know when to leave them. The ideal length—worked out by millennia of use—seems the Collect form. That is why so many of these prayers follow this pattern. The same applies to any Lectionary. The passage, the reflection is to help form a frame of mind, not to produce further phrase-making.

The second optimum in prayer is the right frequency of repetition. Here, too, traditional experience shows that twelve times a year preserves the necessary balance between familiarity and freshness. For the particular value of vocal prayer seems to lie in the fact that it is the expression of a middle state of mind. It lies halfway between an intellectual proposition and an emotional conviction. It is equally composed of rational comprehension and "autosuggestion," the affirmation of the deep will.

These prayers and meditations are then presented in a thirty-one-day pattern. So persevering repetition may yet not cause through monotony, inattention: nor variety of theme result in distraction. As a matter of fact, these aids to a spiritual state of mind were put together mainly for what is called "proximate preparation" for mental prayer. That is to say, they were intended to be used the evening before to assist next day the mind to reflect upon some one aspect of the spiritual life. It is hoped that as these short passages mark points which were reached by an exploring party they may suggest to others to go further and to set down more adequately their findings. For certainly no search is more worth while and no finding of a true seeker but is of value to all.

It may perhaps be thought by a casual reader that the general tone is not sufficiently practical, too contemplative, too little sounding the note of action, intercession, impetration. It may then be repeated that these are the prayers and thoughts of an exploring group of beginners. Prayer must begin with recognition. For worship is an act of estimation. We have to discover, by remaining in His Presence, the nature and will of Him whom we approach. We have to learn one prayer by heart and it certainly takes all a beginner's time, Fiat Voluntas Tua. And when it is learned, is there, can there be anything else to ask?

The initial prayer of each "day" is, in a particular sense, a composition. Those who know the neglected work of that great poet of God the mysterious "Areopagite" (of whom it might well be said that if St. Francis is the lyric poet of Divinity, "Dionysius" was the paeanist), will recognize, framed in Collect form, those tremendous apostrophes whereby this master of adoration creates (as all prayer should) the sense of That which is above and beyond all phrase and all image. By making language confess its final inadequacy, a sense of the word-transcending Reality is flashed on the mind.

The first meditation and the last prayer are by saints both of whom were as intellectual as they were holy and as hard-working as they were other-worldly. St. Albertus Magnus' (or one of his pupil's) concise statement of how to hold on to God and St. Anselm's beautiful prayer of aspiration, seem, the one to open and the other to close so perfectly any attempt to think of God or to draw close to Him, that they have been placed here to bless and in some sense excuse the inadequacy of the rest.

It will be seen that the meditations have tended to distribute themselves roughly into weekly quarters, and that each section begins with vision and ends with practice, opens with outlook and closes with exercise. This seems to be a natural rhythm and one that preserves the necessary constant interrelation between seeing and doing.

Each day's "office" also tends to follow an inherent pattern. The "Dionysian" prayer like the "clef" mark at the start of a musical composition, gives the "key" in which the particular "day's" thought is set: the two first prayers sustain this "direction of aspiration": the meditation itself illustrates this theme (is its libretto, one might say) and the final prayers complete the reflection.

As the tenor of so many of these prayers is the desire to remember constantly the all-pervading, transcendent Presence of God, there have been placed after the first meditation (that on Adherence) and after the Epilogue of Aspiration two hymns. These verses were composed to be sung when the prayers and meditations were being used. The first hymn is constructed from key phrases of "the Areopagite."

The passage from St. Albert (or from one of his pupils) is from the *De Adhaerendo Deo*. That from St. Anselm is from passages in the Preface to his philosophic treatise, *The Proslogion*.

PRAYERS AND MEDITATIONS

I

ADHERENCE

THOU SUPREME GODHEAD, teach us, when we are able to sustain it, the exercise of mystic contemplation, in which we may leave the senses and the activities of the intellect, and all things that the senses and the intellect can perceive, and all things in this world of nothingness, or in that world of being; and, our understanding being laid to rest, may we strive toward an union with Thee whom neither being nor understanding can contain. And by the unceasing and absolute renunciation of ourselves and all things, may we in pureness cast all things aside, and be released from all, and so led upward to the Ray of that divine Darkness which exceedeth all existence.

Ɏ

HAPPY is the man who, by continually effacing all images and through introversion and the lifting up of his mind to God, at last forgets and leaves behind all such hindrances. For by such means only, he operates inwardly, with his naked, pure, simple intellect and affections, about the most pure and simple object,

God. Therefore see that thy whole exercise about God within thee may depend wholly and only on that naked intellect, affection and will. For indeed, this exercise cannot be discharged by any bodily organ, or by the external senses, but only by that which constitutes the essence of man—understanding and love. If, therefore, thou desirest a safe stair and short path to arrive at the end of true bliss, then, with an intent mind, earnestly desire and aspire after continual cleanness of heart and purity of mind. Add to this a constant calm and tranquillity of the senses, and a recollecting of the affections of the heart, continually fixing them above. Work to simplify the heart, that being immovable and at peace from any invading vain phantasms, thou mayest always stand fast in the Lord within thee, to that degree as if thy soul had already entered the always present now of eternity . . . that is, the state of the deity. To mount to God is to enter into oneself. For he who so mounts and enters and goes above and beyond himself, he truly mounts up to God. The mind must then raise itself above itself and say, 'He who above all I need is above all I know.' And so carried into the darkness of the mind, gathering itself into that all-sufficient good, it learns to stay at home and with its whole affection it cleaves and becomes habitually fixed in the supreme good within. Thus continue, until thou becomest immutable and dost arrive at that true life which is God Himself, perpetually, without any vicissitude of space or time, reposing in that inward quiet and secret mansion of the deity."

♆

HYMN

Based on *The Divine Names*
of
DIONYSIUS THE AREOPAGITE

We celebrate by every name
The Nameless All-Transcendent One,
The Boundless Cause from Whose dark Flame
Love's first outpouring was begun.

Creation's vast mysterious fruit,
From star-strewn heaven to humblest clod,
Exists and stems from Thee, the Root,
Intangible, unimaged God.

But Man, creation's curse and boast,
Entrapped in self misunderstood,
Ignores the Truth he longs for most—
Oh free him, All-creative Good!

In secret silence grant release
To wills that strive toward Thee, their Goal,
Thou tranquil Fount of Very Peace
Draw to Thyself each struggling soul.

From senses, feeling, thought, set free
Through blind "Unknowing," flight on flight,
In Darkness make us one with Thee,
Transcendent Archetype of Light!

II

BEING

BOUNDLESS AND BOUNTEOUS SEA of divine Light, may we know in the depths of our own being that Thou art not an attribute of Being, but Being is an attribute of Thee; Thou art not contained in Being but Being is contained in Thee; Thou dost not infuse Being, but Being is infused in Thee. Thou art the Eternity, the Beginning and the Measure of existence, because Thou art the Creative Beginning, Middle and End of all things.

O God, who art Life and Light and Love, who hast given us the life of the body, whereby we are living creatures, the light of the understanding whereby we are human and the love of the heart, whereby we may become divine: Grant that we, living in Thy divine Nature, learning of Thy divine Mind and loving Thy divine kindness, may be united with Thee and, through Thee, with all Thy creatures.

O God, if we seek for Thee because those who fail to find Thee in this dark world are frustrant and lost, Grant this Thy light to that in us which must so seek Thee: If we seek Thee because those who find Thee find all life illuminated and all good things richly to enjoy, Grant these Thy gifts to those who so would love Thee. But if through Thy mercy and Thy doom we seek for Thee in any wise for Thyself then though in this life we never find Thee, deny us not, of Thy compassion, that we be self-consumed with devotion toward Thee as Thou art.

ϒ

GOD *is.* That is the primordial fact. It is in order that we may discover this fact for ourselves, by direct experience, that we exist. The final end and purpose of every human being is the unitive knowledge of God's being.

What is the nature of God's being? The invocation to the Lord's Prayer gives us the answer. "Our Father which *art* in heaven." God is, and is ours—immanent in each sentient being, the life of all lives, the spirit animating every soul. But this is not all. God is also the transcendent Creator and Law-Giver, the Father who loves and, because He loves, also educates His children. And finally, God is "in heaven." That is to say, He possesses a mode of existence which is incommensurable and incompatible with the mode of existence possessed by human beings in their natural, unspiritualized condition. Because He is ours and immanent, God is very close to us. But because He is also in heaven most of us are very far from God. The saint is one who is as close to God as God is close to him.

It is through prayer that men come to the unitive knowledge of God. But the life of prayer is also a life of mortification, or dying to self. It cannot be otherwise; for the more there is of self, the less there is of God. Our pride, our anxiety, our lusts for power and pleasure are God-eclipsing things. So too is that greedy attachment to certain creatures which passes too often for unselfishness and should be called, not altruism, but alter-egoism. And hardly less God-eclipsing is the seemingly self-sacrificing service which we give to any cause or ideal that falls short of the divine. Such service is always idolatry, and makes it impossible for us to worship God as we should, much less to know Him. God's kingdom cannot come unless we begin by making our human kingdoms go. Not only the mad and obviously evil kingdoms, but also the respectable ones—the kingdoms of the scribes and pharisees, the good citizens and pillars of society, no less than the kingdoms of the publicans and sinners. God's being cannot be known by us, if we choose to pay our attention and our allegiance to something else, however creditable that something else may seem in the eyes of the world.

ᛘ

O GOD, who art continually regarding us, our Source, our Goal and our Environment, Grant that we may accept Thee as our Guide: Thou that art continually sustaining us, in whom we live and move and have our being, Grant that we, relying on Thee wholly, may accept Thy offer to be our Providence: Thou that art always informing us, Grant that we may yield to Thy desire to possess us wholly.

Eternal Spirit, most awful, most gentle; most patient, most wise; most loving, least possessive; more pervasive than the air, less noticed, more needed: Let us perceiving Thy gentleness conceive of that awfulness; realizing Thy patience estimate Thy power; experiencing Thy unpossessiveness come to understand the nature of Thy love.

III

AWE

INCOMMUNICABLE, ALL-creative Godhead who surpassest reason, intuition and being; help us to lift up our eyes toward the steep height, and as we strive to ascend unto Thy supernal rays, grant that we may prepare ourselves for the task with holiness and reverent awe.

O Eternal and Infinite Power, may we, meditating on Thee, be delivered from all timidity and weakness; O Eternal and Infinite Wisdom, may we, contemplating Thee, be delivered from all wavering and doubt; O Eternal and Infinite Love, may we, being united with Thee, love our neighbors as ourselves and lose all our self-will in Thy will.

ϒ

FEAR has no part in modern religion. "Religion began with fear," is an old saying. "Free men fear nothing." That, too, is a worn cliché. A saying more to the point is that "perfect love casts out fears." But though no doubt we have cast out the fear of God, it is certainly as doubtful whether we have cast it out by using the above alternative. We may have gotten rid of the fear of God, but we certainly haven't rid ourselves of fear itself. Further, it is equally true that many of our ancestors, who were craven enough to fear God, certainly were outstandingly brave in every other quarter.

What then did they mean by "Godly fear"? "The fear of the Lord is the beginning of wisdom," answers the poet author of Job, after asking, "Where shall wisdom be found?" "Fear Him ye saints, and you will then have nothing else to fear," sang the Scotch Covenanter. Maybe he was not a saint but he was one who proved his proposition as far as courage went.

We admire courage far more than saintliness. Any formula which would make us fearless is then worth our attention. Of course the moment we analyze that key word "fear," we see it is ambiguous. Fear can be used in two completely different senses. The fear that paralyzes never made a man brave, still less wise. What then is Godly fear? We have the word in English—awe. At the start awe always has in it an element of dread. The Covenanter's God was dreadful, no doubt, but He was awful, too. He could be dreaded abjectly, but He could also be adored, worshiped, admired.

It is that element in the Calvinist's creed that kept him from going mad, kept him in a kind of grim exultation. Looking up from the lip of hell to God's unscalable splendor, he certainly was free from such petty concerns as his health, fortune, and personal happiness; the callous burned on his soul made the sting of any earthly misfortune insensible. Wisdom is added to courage when the place which dread took, is filled by reverence. The definition of Deity as *tremendens ac fascinans mysterium*—the awful and spellbinding wonder—goes as near as words can, to holding the essence of awe. The soul is arrested by a splendor so overwhelming that all considerations of safety are driven from the mind.

No doubt such power is not safe: such experience is not sedative. But in spite of the danger, the exploring soul is drawn on. "Yea, though He slay me still must I trust in Him, still must I go to Him." Such awe is always liberating, always ennobling, always energizing. For it is closely akin to that selfless adoration of unbearable beauty, which cauterizes with ecstasy the slack empty soul. Then, once we have realized something, the slightest something, of what God may be in Himself, the fretful concern with ourselves and the superstitious degrading of Him to an attentive provider of our comforts, leaves us for good. We are freed, by our admiration of a stupendous wonder, in the presence of which we feel the liberating sense of our own insignificance.

So, out of awe, true love can grow, and we can begin to conceive how He who is the transcendent, because He *is* truly transcendent, cannot but be immanent. He has, by making us have awe of Him, delivered us from ourselves and made Himself real to us. In this way, and in no other, could we have come to deliverance from self and trust in Him. Both are impossible so long as we treat

Him as a convenience, as a means to our happiness. We had to believe first that He was wholly alien to us to learn how much more deeply than we could love and know ourselves, He loved and knew our true nature, His nature in us. Then, as dread was transmuted into awe, so awe turns into love—the love which can annihilate fear because this love so draws the soul out of itself that the soul only desires to find its every limit annihilated in God.

ALMIGHTY GOD, grant unto us Thy creatures, some apprehension of Thy stupendous splendor, that we being raised by inexhaustible wonder, may be delivered from the separateness of our selfhood through the contemplation of Thy perfect and all-transcending unity.

O Transcendent Splendor, lift up our eyes, we beseech Thee, from the false lights of the world, that we being radiated by Thy invisible glory, may be transmuted into that which Thou wouldst have us be.

O Thou before whom all imagining staggers and is felled; at whose dark boundaries comprehension can only bow in helplessness and surrender; help us to remember that we can never know Thee until we love Thee above all else.

IV

FAITH

O MYSTERIOUS ORIGIN OF ALL origin, and bounteous Communication (so far as such may be) of hidden mysteries; even as things which are intellectually discerned cannot be comprehended or perceived by means of those things which belong to the senses, nor simple and imageless things by means of types and images; by the same law of truth Thy boundless super-essence surpasses essence and Thy super-intellectual unity surpasses intelligences. Teach us, we pray, in silent awareness, with the key of Unknowing to unlock our finite natures to Thy infinite mystery.

O God who has enfolded us in the veil of this life that it may be to us both trial and opportunity, Grant, that we realizing our blindness and proneness to illusion, may, by our ever more frequent turning to Thee, be permitted never to lose hold upon Thee, though we may not yet see Thee; until, by the constant and patient walk with Thee in the darkness, we may be prepared and enabled to endure beholding Thy glory, face to face.

O Thou who art as compassionate as Thou art powerful, as wise as Thou art just: Grant us the faith fully to believe in Thee; the strength unwaveringly to adhere to Thee and the will to be wholly lost in Thy will.

♆

FAITH, in our Western tradition, is the initial step in the three stages that lead through hope to love. Without faith we are hopeless and loveless. But faith today is modern man's chief stumbling block. In the Eastern tradition knowledge, not faith, is the first step. Yet it is only because we have used faith in a mistaken sense, that there seems to be a conflict between these two presentations of the eternal gospel. Faith, in fact, is right knowledge. For faith is not believing something which our intelligence denies. It is the choice of the nobler hypothesis. Faith is the resolve to place the highest meaning on the facts which we observe.

It is erroneous to say that science is based on doubt, and religion on credulity. Science, too, is based on faith—it chooses to believe that the universe works by regular laws, and when exceptions appear, science believes (and has proved wise in believing) that further knowledge will not destroy but enlarge the faith in law. But science confines itself to a smaller range of facts than we have to confront in our ordinary lives. No man can live without *any* meaning to order his incessant experiences. If he fails consciously to make his own hypothesis as to the meaning of life he will invariably accept without thought that hypothesis which prevails in his society.

A man lives more deeply and more truly the

more he can creatively make meaning of his experiences. When he embraces every experience —pain, loss, death, his subconscious, the apparently random acts of nature or of his fellow creatures—then he can endure all, and not only endure, but give a creative response, and re-create. His faith has made him whole, and becoming whole, he can create around him wholeness.

The one meaning which will co-ordinate every possible experience, is God. The most meaningful hypothesis is that behind the apparent muddle of multiplicity, is One. That hypothesis proves its correctness both by ordering our outer experience so that we can understand it, and also by making it possible for us to live so that we can take an ever-increasingly constructive part in that Whole.

Faith, then, is no call for a leap in the dark. On the contrary, it is urging us to face two facts: firstly, that everyone must have some meaning, some hypothesis, in which to frame his experiences —otherwise he can only be imbecile, with no consistent response to anything; and secondly, that as we must have some meaning we may as well have one that embraces everything. We can see that it is those men and women who have had the vitality to choose the largest possible meaning whose lives have proved most co-ordinated and creative, most happy for themselves, most blessed for others.

Faith, therefore, is the right knowledge that chooses to arrange all experience in that vast framework of meaning called the Will of God. If we bring all our experience within that comprehensive design we shall find that we are able increasingly to make a creative response to every event, every contingency. But to do so requires a life of great vitality. It requires a life in which nothing is admitted, either in action or interest, and finally not even in thought, which would conflict with the supreme all-embracing purpose. The faith to believe and to live as though there were meaning in each momentary event is crowned in the end with the power to see that there is no chance or accident.

The amount of meaning that anyone can see in life depends on how much he wishes to see, and is ready to pay the price of seeing, by giving up all wishes for smaller selfish meanings, and the degree to which he is ready to accept the consequence of his acts by rejecting wholly that blasphemous alibi which pleads that "Life is a tale told by an idiot."

ᛘ

O GOD who has granted us the incomparable privilege that we may be aware, through faith, of Thy awful illumination and liberating Presence, so that we may perceive the meaning of every instant, if we will, and thus be freed from any absorption of anxiety, of greed or of self-will: Grant, that we being constantly re-created by this Thy love, may henceforth live no longer in the false life of self-love, but in Thee, and through Thee in all Thy creatures.

O God who of Thy wisdom has in this life denied us certitude, until our wills are wholly in accord with Thine, Grant that we may humbly confess to this our ignorance, not claiming an infallibility or information that Thou hast not given us, until, by submission and our willingness to wait upon Thee, Thou mayest guide us into Thy perfect light, where with all the blessed, we may henceforward enjoy the supreme blessedness of knowing wholly Thy will and performing it fully.

V

HOPE

UNUTTERABLE AND NAMELESS Godhead, give us grace to hope in Thee beyond the whole created universe, knowing that Thy formless nature produces all-form, that in Thee alone not-being is an excess of Being, lifelessness an excess of Life, and Thy mindless state an excess of Wisdom. Thus striving to express Thy divine attributes in a transcendent manner by the help of negative images, may we hope to draw ever nearer to Thy imageless Reality.

O God, our ignorance of Thee is beyond all thought, our need of Thee beyond all words, but we believe that Thou dost answer in ways that we cannot understand, the desire for Thee which we cannot express. We would silently thank Thee for Thy mercy and unresistingly accept Thy salvation.

O God whose wisdom is too wide for the span of our narrow minds, whose love too vast for our timid hearts to embrace: Grant that we, knowing increasingly our ignorance, may fall back upon Thy infinite knowledge, and, by the very failing of our natural heart and courage, be compelled to accept the loving offer of Thy sustaining grace.

ᛘ

BECAUSE we have misunderstood the meaning of faith we tend, too, to misunderstand hope, the second of the three virtues which lead us to God. "By hope are we saved," says St. Paul. We thought it was faith that saved. True, faith does begin our salvation; but being saved is a threefold process. Faith reaches out to salvation; hope touches it; charity holds it fast. Faith is our philosophy—our deliberate decision to give the highest possible meaning to our multiplicity of experiences, and to co-ordinate them all under one embracing law. Hope is the necessary next step. Hope is the personal application of our philosophy of faith. Faith is the root, hope is the flower, charity is the fruit—the three are one. Without the deep root of faith that in the nature of things there lies meaning, hope will wither, and charity will never grow.

"The universe means well by you," says faith; and hope replies, "I will co-operate, believing that the meaning and the Meaner are so great and wise that even my minuteness is meant to count in the whole. I have now the highest reasonable expectation, a 'sure and certain hope,' that if I act on my belief that life has meaning, the supreme Maker of meaning will bring me within His meaning and make me a partaker in making it manifest. He, and He alone, has made meaning of the tangled skein of my private experience."

God saves us from ourselves. He saves us from despair at finding no meaning in ourselves. He saves us by showing us that we can lose ourselves in His unlimited meaning. And this is no private salvation. A man of faith has hope not only for himself, but for all men in every pass and circumstance. For He has assured us that He will never cease encompassing and drawing out each and every soul until there is not one that, despairing of finding meaning in itself, but turns and asks Him to give it the meaning it must have. He will force no one, for no one can be forced to see meaning. But in His divine love He has made every mind, so that, while it is free to delay until the end of time, in the end it must and can only find its meaning and fulfillment in Him.

Therefore to faith we must add hope, the sure hope that God's waiting is not indifference, but love, the love that will enable the whole groaning and travailing creation to achieve, through faith and hope, a new birth of charity. This is the state of creative love which enables the creature to acknowledge that from faith and through hope a new creation is being won, which will make all the present suffering and the endurance sustained against cynicism and despair, incomparably worth while.

♆

O GOD, whenever we forget Thee, then may our heart lose its hope, our mind forget its meaning, our will its grasp. For in Thee alone have we sure hope, in Thy purpose alone may we find meaning and in Thy love only may our hearts find invincible courage.

O God our hope, now that we look toward Thee we know that though we are blind and cannot see Thee, Thou art regarding us and enlightening us in the depth of our mind: Now that we are listening for Thee, Thou art speaking to us, and, though we are deaf and cannot hear Thy voice, Thou art instructing our deepest will. Our cry is the echo of Thy call to us. Now that we are striving to hold to Thee, though we are numb and cannot feel Thy touch, Thou art sustaining us: now that we are attempting to draw close to Thee, Thou art drawing us to Thyself.

VI

CHARITY

THOU WHO ART THE SUPREME Fount and Producer of Unity, the great attractive Power uniting things that are sundered, may Thy infinite charity draw all creatures unto Thyself for their perfect fruition in union with each other and with Thee.

O God whose love is knowledge and whose knowledge is love, grant unto us that we knowing truthfully our neighbor's nature and task, may love cordially what through that problem and capacity Thou hast decreed he shall become, so that he also so loving us in truth in Thee, we may together come to that unity of the spirit wherein we may even here enjoy the blessed community of those who are constantly aware of Thy reconciling presence.

O God may our confidence in Thee equal our mistrust of ourselves; our reliance in Thy power, our misgiving at our own weakness, our hope in Thy wisdom, our evidence of our ignorance, our faith in Thy love, our despair at our lovelessness. So that we, knowing Thee in Thy creative, redemptive and sanctifying power, goodness and wisdom may discard this false selfhood of ignorance and be restored to Thy perfect eternal nature.

♆

CHARITY is an end term. It is the fruit. Without the root of faith, grounded in right knowledge, and the flower of hope in which the fruit forms, true love is impossible. Love, that does not spring from faith and hope, is sentimentality. When we have learned that the world has meaning and that we ourselves may, with a reasonable hope, be part of that meaning, then love is a consequence, an inevitable consequence. And that love is both a return and a gift. It is a return, a spontaneous offering, a lifting up of the heart in gratitude when we realize what we have found. The best is truest: there is a friend behind the phenomena.

That the universe has complete meaning and that we, if we choose, can have an integral part in that meaning, fills the heart with an irresistible relief. Charity is not first of all something which we ought to feel toward our fellows. It is, first and foremost, something we may, and must feel toward God Himself. If we never felt this gratitude and love toward God we are unlikely ever to be able truly to love our fellows. We have one thing which God has alienated from Himself that we might have the right of giving, as the proof of our love—to Him we can offer ourselves with real devotion. We are given this right—to love and bless our Maker, our Friend infinitely kind and wise.

But that is not all that God bestows on His children. The divine charity makes us able on our scale to be creative, to undertake part of the creative and redemptive work, if we but offer our love to Him. Through our love of God we become capable of loving, and not merely patronizing, our fellow man. For God who loves us and daily proves His love for us by provision and by forgiveness, loves all His creation equally, and would have us love in the same unlimited way. The faith that shows us there is meaning, the hope that finds place for us in that vast pattern of purpose —this faith and hope also include all our fellows, and call us to see that their relation to God is the same as our relation to Him. If they already see this, then we can mutually acknowledge our relationship as His fellow children. If they have yet to see it, then He calls us to His task, to win them to this love-awakening knowledge.

For as He, who has all power, denies Himself any power over us save that of love, to win us to love and obedience, so He would have us use the same power whereby He has won us to Himself. This is not sentimentality. On the contrary it is a hard saying. For, because God out of love will never coerce man, will never use any power but love to turn man back to Himself; man is free to torture and torment himself until he sees that his methods are not those of his Maker.

Nor is that all; because God will win man by love alone, He permits those who love, to endure the mistaken actions of those who are still denying love as the principle of the universe. This can only look like callous and hideous injustice unless in that vicarious suffering the creature sees itself called on to be a creator with God, through using His creative power of forgiveness and love. No smaller construction of the world's agony can make sense of the actual experience and apparent hideous injustice which happen when men deny love, and believing that the universe is indifferent to them, hope with violence and cunning to establish justice and mercy.

ᛘ

O GOD who has revealed to us that of all the virtues, Love may for us most clearly describe Thy infinite nature and that when we selflessly love we approach most nearly to Thy Presence: Grant us therefore this the supreme virtue; for Thou hast shown us that, without it, persistence hardens into pride, peace chills to cold-heartedness and even humility sinks to despair: But enkindled by loving-kindness all these virtues become alive bearing us up into Thy presence where alone our hearts may rest.

O God grant that what we believe to be our love for what we imagine Thee to be may become suspect to our conscience should such a love check or chill in anywise our love for Thy beloved children, our fellow creatures.

VII

OBEDIENCE

WE PRAY THEE TO TEACH US TO worship with reverent silence the unutterable Truths, and with the unfathomable and holy veneration of our minds, to approach that Mystery of Godhead which exceeds all mind and being.

O Forgiving Father, who never weariest of our repentance, Grant that we realizing this, Thy blessed nature, may constantly lay hold of Thy everlasting mercy and so obtain the grace to begin once more.

O God, who of Thy great mercy hast brought us to the knowledge of the supreme destiny for which Thou hast made us and to which Thou hast called us: Grant, we beseech Thee that we may not be disobedient to that call or slack in conforming with that guidance and leading, but that in total dedication of life, of thought, word and deed, we may by Thy grace be permitted, even here, to enter into that knowledge of Thee, which is the life eternal.

ᛘ

HOLY obedience is a religious phrase almost as unpopular as Godly fear. It is of course the third, the mental discipline which completes the medieval triad of spiritual training, the other two of which are the discipline of the individual's economy by poverty, and of his body by chastity.

We have rejected all three. But they stood for something, and sometimes achieved an outstanding change in human nature. Can we then find the abiding essentials behind these phrases? Continence (something far wider, less rigid and yet more exacting than chastity) would seem to be the principle underlying what, in chastity, is simply a particular and exceptional expression. Frugality—the determination to ration all one's living—is the deep and sound principle of which poverty, which begs to live by others' toil, is only an exceptional development.

And so, coming to obedience, we can see that it is merely one method of attaining anonymity, selflessness. To hand one's resources to him who begs for help because he has failed to provide for himself, and then oneself to beg from him who has succeeded in providing for himself, may be one's own salvation, but not a social solution. So, too, to obey the will of another in order to curb one's own, is a private, not a general answer to the danger of the will to power. Holy obedience can only be given to God.

But can it be given directly? Must not God grant us a surrogate to whom we pay His due?

The choice between "dogmatic authority" or "antinomian libertinage" is, however, not final. God Himself has given us a universal law witnessed by the Church Universal. That law is the Two Commandments. There remains, however, the problem of how to fulfill them, apply them, obey them in every contingency.

There can be no doubt that the learning how to fulfill these vast principles, is slow work. It is, however, a task which cannot be handed over to another. We may and ought to be helped by the advice, encouragement, judgment, and criticism of those who are in advance of us. But they cannot take over our souls. Our free will is God's particular unique gift to each of us, the raison d'être of our creation, our essential being and responsibility which He never permits us to alienate.

Holy obedience is, then, not to arrest and infantalize the soul. On the contrary, it is to train the soul in two things: firstly, in those skilled applications of the general law to the particular issues. By this skill the soul grows in controlled freedom. Secondly, by that growing sensitiveness to God's will the soul at length may attain to actual guidance. By such obedience the soul develops, for it is in this ever more patient observance that it finds that God's service is indeed perfect freedom.

But to find that free obedience there must be a great patience and promptitude. Unless we leave our lives carefully free of distractions and prejudices, we shall not be able to notice, far less to respond to, those sensitive leadings whereby

God would teach us. We must clear our circumstances, our minds, and indeed our bodies, if we would be able to follow those leadings and be able to take those openings. The spirit of God will never shout down our self-will. Holy obedience is shown in that readiness, that mobility, that freedom from adhesions and inertia, which permit us to respond to these sensitive guidances. God teaches holy obedience far more often by asking us questions than by giving us orders. He, then, who would be guided, will always be in a state of readiness to listen to such questions, and also in a state of humility to know that not till many years will he be able to answer each question as fully and as freely as God would have him answer. But every attempt to respond leads to a greater freedom of response, to a more constructive and creative answer next time.

When the soul has reached such readiness and openness that it is prepared to realize that there is no chance or accident, then in every circumstance large and small, and in every split second it can hear the voice of God asking it whether it wishes to do His will. Holy obedience and the whole spiritual life is in the end all a matter of will. And once the will is prepared to find God's will He then shows it how it may fulfill that will. Once again we learn that only in His service and by obeying Him, can we be not only free, but also at last become children of His nature, creating as He intends that we should create.

ᛘ

GRANT us, O God, the supreme gift to be able to ask freely to be given nothing, because we have been granted to know that as little as by adding our power to Thine could we hope to help Thee, so as little can our insight suggest to Thy wisdom courses however minute, that Thou hadst not already planned, or our love prompt Thee to a further compassion that Thou mightest yet feel toward the least or most perverse of Thy creatures.

Lord of the universe, obedience to Thy will is not submission to a harsh law but participation in a divine dance. Thou dost not ask that we blindly conform but trustingly swing into the unfolding design. At every inner prompting of Thy spirit grant that we may truly obey, and with faith and courage and humility forget ourselves in unhesitating desire to be used for Thy creative purposes.

Grant to us, O God, the grace of resignation and desire for Thee, that our every thought, word and deed may conform in perfect obedience to Thy will.

VIII

TRUTH

DIVINE AND INEFFABLE TRUTH teach us to know that all is well with him who is united unto Thee, even though the multitude reprove him as one out of his mind, not perceiving that he is but come out of an erring mind unto the Truth through right faith. And let us verily know that instead of being, as they say, distraught, he hath been relieved from the unstable ever-changing movements which tossed him hither and thither in the mazes of error, and hath been set at liberty through the simple and unchanging Truth.

O God we implore Thee grant us to gain the knowledge of Thee, although that mean that we lose knowledge, interest and skill in all else: Grant us to gain the knowledge of ourself, although this mean that we lose our present will to live. For only if we can come truly to know Thee can we cease to love the creatures more than Thee. And only if we can truly know ourselves can we cease from that deadly self-love whereby we are debarred from Thy eternal Life.

O God as Thou art That which by Thy mercy thou hast shown us Thy nature to be, Grant us to know why, though we have this saving knowledge we still continue as we are; grant us to understand why we still fall into forgetfulness and revert to ways of thought, word and deed arising from our disproved ignorance: teach us why it is that though our minds acknowledge Thee, our wills are yet unable to submit wholly and cheerfully to Thine.

ᛘ

WITH beauty and goodness, truth makes up our temporal apprehension of God. And as love and beauty throw light on each other, so that we can see that they are radiated out from a common source, so does truth throw light on them both, and is in turn illuminated by both of them. Yet it is harder for us to meditate on truth, than on beauty or love. For truth seems clear, obvious, harsh. There are no iridescent fringes of romance about it. Truth isn't for meditation, to give us awe: it is for use, to make us more canny.

But truth is a "mystery"—quite as much a "mystery" as is beauty. God is indicated in truth as much as He is in beauty. Why it is hard for us to see that, is because during the modern age we have not been very truthful about truth. Hence in religion we have been afraid of facts. The good and the beautiful weren't really true. The true wasn't good or beautiful. The ideal meant no longer utter enduring reality behind all shifting appearances. It had become the polite word for the unreal. You'd better face up to what is. This is a world of iron law. The life in you is one of blind struggle. And you yourself are a lonely spark quite sundered from the others, and soon to be quenched in the universal blackness. You live and die alone. Those are the hard facts, we say, and now let us have a little camouflage and gilding put on them by ideals, and values, and aesthetics.

But these are *not* the facts. Let us be truthful. Neither Calvin nor mechanism is true—let alone good or beautiful. What are the facts about where we are, what we are, and who we are? This is a world of lawful freedom—of iron mechanism no conclusive evidence has ever been found. The life within us is one which has advanced not by brutal struggle, but by creative choice, awareness and sensitiveness: our consciousness is not cut off, but communes ceaselessly, below the level of our egotism, with unnumbered others. These are the truthful facts, and they are facts which make for the growth of the soul, if we act on them. How, then, have we so misapprehended, how did we get into this tangle over truth? Because we wanted to have a useful, convenient truth, and that is to sin against pure truth. At first it was highly convenient to believe that the universe didn't care what we did, that life compelled us to act only in our own interests, and that each of us was only and really a separate self. Later on, when we found that we couldn't get on with such wishful thinking, it was not such fun. But that is always so. For greed leads to fear, and fear to ignorance.

We must, then, start afresh by being more honest about truth. It is far from easy. For, first, if life has an objective meaning, then we must act up to it always—not merely when we find that we are not enjoying ourselves when we try to serve only ourselves. If this world and life are conditions under which men may learn moral action, then we must act morally and to act otherwise is to frustrate all one's living. Secondly, we have to learn to perceive meaning in every moment and every event.

He who would see truth everywhere, must himself be truthful. He must not only be accurate about detail often so minute as not to excite powerful emotion; he must also have overcome all his prejudices. He must have gotten rid of all his pretensions. He must have achieved complete anonymity. That is why the saints have laid such stress upon being absolutely, selflessly truthful. That is why any religion which permits, out of traditional cowardice, a conflict to arise between its dogmas and absolute truthfulness, always ruins its spiritual life. For if we are, however slightly, dishonest, we cannot pray. God is the God of truth. Only those that want to know reality for no other reason than that they may know the truth, only the single-hearted, may see God.

Truth, then, like beauty, begins by demanding that if we would love it, we must ask no return, and seek no convenience. And when, in order to follow it, we have sacrificed what we clung to and were, we find that truth, as does beauty, transforms those who so surrender and lose themselves, into beings of power and loveliness, that they may truthfully be called by the most beautiful of titles, Sons of God.

♆

(A prayer for spiritual tact)

O GOD who sustains the whole visible world by Thy invisible unobtrusive touch so that its vast manifested presence must vanish away were for a moment that support withdrawn: Grant that we may so touch the flow of events that we may neither be carried away by them nor strive to wrest them to our own purposes. But, taught by Thee, how to touch without deforming, guide without obtruding and sustain without imposing, we may by Thy grace be prevented from obstructing any one of those who seek to find in Thee their sole guide and sustainer.

O God, who hast made us long for the transparent clarity of Thy utter truth; help us to slough off our blurred and narrowed vision of things, in which we have wrapped ourselves for safety, and asking Thee for the grace of courage may we step forth in simplicity to meet whatever impact of Thy truth Thou dost send to set us free.

IX

BEAUTY (I)

 THOU BEAUTIFUL! THOU ART the beginning of all things, as being the Creative Cause, who of Thy great goodness hast created us a little lower than the angels. Grant us grace to press on in prayer, looking upward toward those Angelic Intelligences, burnished mirrors, bright, untarnished, without spot or blemish, who receive all Thy beauty, and kindle within themselves (so far as may be) with unalloyed radiance, the Goodness of the Secret Silence.

O Eternal Light, radiate us away, that we being emptied of everything but Thee, Thy presence may be manifest in all and through all.

O Thou who alone canst deliver us from our ourselves, reveal Thyself, that we seeing the beauty of Thy perfect liberty may be released from the deadly imprisonment to our self-love and enter into Thy eternal freedom.

ϒ

BEAUTY arises when the parts of a whole are related to one another and to the totality in a manner which we apprehend as orderly and significant. But the first principle of order is God, and God is the final, deepest meaning of all that exists. God, then, is manifest in the relationship which makes things beautiful. He resides in that lovely interval which harmonizes events on all the planes, where we discover beauty. We apprehend Him in the alternate voids and fullnesses of a cathedral; in the spaces that separate the salient features of a picture; in the living geometry of a flower, a sea shell, an animal; in the pauses and intervals between the notes of music, in their differences of tone and sonority; and finally, on the plane of conduct, in the love and gentleness, the confidence and humility, which give beauty to the relationships between human beings.

Such, then, is God's beauty, as we apprehend it in the sphere of created things. But it is also possible for us to apprehend it, in some measure at least, as it is in itself. The beatific vision of divine beauty is the knowledge, so to say, of pure interval, of harmonious relationship apart from the things related. A material figure of beauty-in-itself is the cloudless evening sky, which we find inexpressibly lovely, although it possesses no orderliness of arrangement, since there are no distinguishable parts to be harmonized. We find it beautiful because it is an emblem of the infinite clear light of the void. To the knowledge of this pure interval we shall come only when we have learnt to mortify attachment to creatures, above all to ourselves.

Moral ugliness arises when self-assertion spoils the harmonious relationship which should exist between sentient beings. Analogously, aesthetic and intellectual ugliness arise when one part in a whole is excessive or deficient. Order is marred, meaning distorted and, for the right, the divine relation between things or thoughts, there is substituted a wrong relation—a relationship that manifests symbolically, not the immanent and transcendent source of all beauty, but that chaotic disorderliness which characterizes creatures when they try to live independently of God.

Ψ

O GOD grant us to see every beauty of character, every aspect of sincerity, every expression of loving-kindness, in those who are repelled by our meanness, censure and insincerity, who resent our uncharitableness and are embittered by our complaining. Forgive us for so deeply offending them and making hard their approach to Thee. And grant us to be healed of these our blemishes through the admiration that Thou canst give us for the graces Thou hast granted them.

Thou, who dost know in Thy never-flagging love for us that we may sometimes be drawn to seek for Thee by finding traces of Thy beauty, and so hast scattered Thy clues throughout the universe with ceaseless prodigality; give us grace so to respond to these signalings from Thee, that we may press on from beauty to beauty, never resting until we come into Thy very presence, beauty inexpressible!

X

LOVE

OVE, THOU ALL-POWERFUL Foundation of all things maintaining and embracing the universe, founding and establishing and compacting it; knitting the whole together in Thyself without a rift, producing the universe out of Thyself as out of an all-powerful Root, and attracting all things back again unto Thyself; cast on us all Thy voluntary yoke and sweet travail of divine all-powerful and indestructible desire for Thy goodness.

O Thou that art Light and Life and Love: Grant us the wisdom to see clearly what we should do: the vitality to perform fully what we perceive: and the devotion that rejoices that it is permitted to do Thy will on earth as it is in Heaven.

O Thou, who art Beauty, Truth, Love and Holiness: bring us to an ever deeper composure in and through Thy beauty; to an ever closer correspondence in and through Thy truth; an ever wider interest and sympathy in and through Thy kindness; and finally to that utter wholeness in Thee through Thy eternal and most blessed unity.

ψ

GOD is love, and there are blessed moments when even to unregenerate human beings it is granted to know Him as love. But it is only in the saints that this knowledge becomes secure and continuous. By those in the earlier stages of the spiritual life God is apprehended predominantly as law. It is through obedience to God the Law-Giver that we come at last to know God the loving Father.

The law which we must obey, if we would know God as love, is itself a law of love. "Thou shalt love God with all thy soul, and with all thy heart, with all thy mind and with all thy strength. And thou shalt love thy neighbor as thyself." We cannot love God as we should, unless we love our neighbors as we should. We cannot love our neighbors as we should, unless we love God as we should. And, finally, we cannot realize God as the active, all-pervading principle of love, until we ourselves have learnt to love Him and our fellow creatures.

Idolatry consists in loving a creature more than we love God. There are many kinds of idolatry, but all have one thing in common: namely, self-love. The presence of self-love is obvious in the grosser forms of sensual indulgence, or the pursuit of wealth and power and praise. Less manifestly, but none the less fatally, it is present in our inordinate affections for individuals, persons, places, things and institutions. And even in men's most heroic sacrifices to high causes and noble ideals, self-love has its tragic place. For when we sacrifice ourselves to any cause or ideal that is lower than the highest, less than God Himself, we are merely sacrificing one part of our unregenerate being to another part which we and other people regard as more creditable. Self-love still persists, still prevents us from obeying perfectly the first of the two great commandments. God can be loved perfectly only by those who have killed out the subtlest, the most nobly sublimated forms of self-love. When this happens, when we love God as we should and therefore know God as love, the tormenting problem of evil ceases to be a problem, the world of time is seen to be an aspect of eternity, and in some inexpressible way, but no less really and certainly, the struggling, chaotic multiplicity of life is reconciled in the unity of the all-embracing divine charity.

ᛘ

O LOVE of God in whose fire the iron of resentment is melted from our hearts: O light of God, whose beam pierces the fog of the willful ignorance in our minds: O will of God, in whose hold our fractured wills are knit: kindle us, illuminate us, embrace us and make us whole in Thee.

O God who alone knowest the weakness of those that love Thee and the false strength of those who love themselves: Grant to us some freedom from ourselves that we, at last loving Thee truly, may be enabled to love one another as Thou hast loved us.

XI

GRACE (I)

NKNOWABLE AND BLINDING Goodness, give us the grace to know that with undeviating power Thou givest Thyself for the deification of those that turn to Thee.

O God who by Thy power, wisdom and love always sustains us, fully and immediately in Thy presence; by Thy mercy grant that we may never cease to be aware of this our relationship with Thee and by Thy prevailing grace so assist our wills that they may therefore always be in accord with Thine.

Grant us O Lord we beg the blessed gift of that interior silence which arises from an entire acceptance of Thy blessed will, that we may hold our peace, as part of Thy perfect ever-creative peace and so be enabled to be still, though knowing that Thou indeed art God.

✝

GRACES are the free gifts of help bestowed by God upon each one of us, in order that we may be assisted to achieve our final end and purpose; namely, unitive knowledge of divine reality. Such helps are very seldom so extraordinary that we are immediately aware of their true nature as God-sends. In the overwhelming majority of cases they are so inconspicuously woven into the texture of common life, that we do not know that they are graces, unless and until we respond to them as we ought, and so receive the material, moral or spiritual benefits, which they were meant to bring us. If we do not respond to these ordinary graces as we ought, we shall receive no benefit and remain unaware of their nature or even of their very existence. Grace is always sufficient, provided we are ready to co-operate with it. If we fail to do our share, but rather choose to rely on self-will and self-direction, we shall not only get no help from the graces bestowed upon us; we shall actually make it impossible for further graces to be given. When used with an obstinate consistency, self-will creates a private universe walled off impenetrably from the light of spiritual reality; and within these private universes the self-willed go their way, unhelped and unillumined, from accident to random accident, or from calculated evil to calculated evil. It is of such that St. Francis de Sales is speaking when he says, "God did not deprive thee of the operation of his love, but thou didst deprive His love of thy co-operation. God would never have rejected thee, if thou hadst not rejected Him."

To be clearly and constantly aware of the divine guidance is given only to those who are already far advanced in the life of the spirit. In its earlier stages we have to work, not by the direct perception of God's successive graces, but by faith in their existence. We have to accept as a working hypothesis that the events of our lives are not merely fortuitous, but deliberate tests of intelligence and character, specially devised occasions (if properly used) for spiritual advance. Acting upon this working hypothesis, we shall treat no occurrence as intrinsically unimportant. We shall never make a response that is inconsiderate, or a mere automatic expression of our self-will, but always give ourselves time, before acting or speaking, to consider what course of behavior would seem to be most in accord with the will of God, most charitable, most conducive to the achievement of our final end. When such becomes our habitual response to events, we shall discover, from the nature of their effects, that some at least of these occurrences were divine graces in the disguise sometimes of trivialities, sometimes of inconveniences or even of pains and trials. But if we fail to act upon the working hypothesis that grace exists, grace will in effect be nonexistent as far as we are concerned. We shall prove by a life of accident at the best, or, at the worst, of downright evil, that God does not help human beings, unless they first permit themselves to be helped.

ᛘ

O GOD, every perfect thing comes down from Thee; every virtue is Thy gift, not our achievement: Grant us therefore humility without its self-regarding shadow despair: trust without presumption of self-conceit; love without possessiveness or any jealousy; strength without dominance; gentleness without weakness.

O God, as a seedling receives the nourishment of sun and rain; help us to receive in our hearts Thy grace, which Thou art offering to us at every moment.

XII

PURITY

INTANGIBLE AND UNIMAGED God, who exceedest all things in a superessential manner and art revealed in Thy naked truth to those alone who pass right through the opposition of good and evil, and pass beyond the topmost altitudes of the holy ascent and leave behind them all divine enlightenment and voices and heavenly utterances and plunge into the Darkness where Thou truly dwellest, grant us that utter purification, and then grant us Thy truth, O Thou who art beyond all things.

Father, who hast given us this body and this event as the only vehicle and way to Thee, grant that we being enabled to recognize this Thy loving wisdom both in provision and in inspiration, in instrument and in task, may use them always and only for this Thy divine purpose.

O God of Thy forgiving mercy never cease to instruct us in that blessed discipline whereby we may attain to our incomparable goal, union with Thee: Frame our minds, that all our thoughts may refer to Thy comprehensive understanding: Fill our hearts with courageous loving-kindness:

Align our wills to the patience of Thy undeflectible purpose: until, in all our activities we have learned to wait upon Thee and in every endurance we may know that we are doing Thy will.

ϒ

PURE mountain air; a deep pool of pure water; a pure and flawless crystal—these are faint reflections of that absolute purity which is beneath the shifting multiplicity of things. It is as if an infinite expanse of profound silence and light were stained by changing colors and disturbed by snatches of sound. They disguise the depths below and confuse us when we try to enter into the meaning of purity.

Purity has two aspects for us—a negative and a positive. As we look up from our sinful and limited selves toward God's vast and untouched purity, we seem to be facing mere emptiness. We shudder and draw back. "Nothingness" is a concept uncongenial to the human desire-laden heart and the human image-ridden mind. But if we have courage resolutely to keep on gazing, although we may still see nothing in the background, in the foreground we begin to see old familiar things in an entirely new and different way. In that seemingly empty continuum they appear as they are, undistorted by our notions and desires. And if we continue our steady gaze, praying for grace and courage to see further, there will sooner or later swim into view, projected against that incomprehensible clarity, the monstrous constructions of the ego. We see our multiple selves as we are. Few can endure that vision for long. It can only be taken in small doses. But it is a necessary purgation if we are ever to find our feet on the bedrock foundation of humility. From there alone can we safely look up into transcendent purity, so far beyond our reach as to seem utterly void, the negation of all that we have known.

To see the positive aspect of purity we must look within. If we are patient and "wait on the Lord," He will open the inner gate and show us, behind all we can call our own, the pure essence of our being. It is nothing that we have made or earned or deserved or can in any way claim, and yet it is our central core without which we should cease to be at all. It is the source of life, the well-spring of creative power. Ashvagosha, the Buddhist saint, calls it the pure essence of mind which is ultimate purity, the quintessence of truth. Its inner activity brings about harmony, simplicity and unity. Of the same substance are those angelic intelligences which Dionysius the Areopagite compares to burnished mirrors without spot or blemish. If we could only be humble and persistent enough to penetrate "this muddy vesture of decay" which so effectively bars us from the mystery within our own souls, we might glimpse even now at rare illuminated moments the positive significance of purity. Compared with the energy of purposed wisdom and love pouring through at those moments, our self-devised scheming and possessive affections appear negative indeed! Yet positive purity is not an end in itself. It attracts us with silent irresistible power to look beyond itself. It is only a medium for vision. "Blessed are the pure in heart for they shall see God," and seeing Him within and without as one Truth, whole and perfect, they no longer have even a glance to spare for the old half-real fragments of separate half-seen truths.

ᛘ

O GOD we do not ask for anything but deliverance from demandingness: for forgiveness from having made ourselves creatures that are continually craving for self-satisfactions: for lasting redemptions from ourselves by that cleansing from all selfhood which alone is the purity of heart that will permit us to see Thee.

Almighty God, may the living flame of Thy purity burn away those unwholesome mists of self-concern which lead us astray and overcloud our resolve to give our whole heart to Thee.

XIII

HUMILITY

ALL-TRANSCENDENT GODHEAD, not only infinite Greatness but Smallness is attributed to Thy nature because it is outside all solidity and distance and penetrates unhindered into all things and through all things, energizing in and reaching to the dividing of soul and spirit; and being a Discerner of the desires and thoughts of the heart. Thy smallness is irrepressible, infinite, unlimited, and while comprehending all things is itself incomprehensible.

Teach us to sink in wondering humility before Thy smallness!

This is our prayer: O God, if Thou shouldst go over this dust in passing to another soul, where Thou hast trod, O may we trust, there may remain for it, in it, a glow.

(Anonymity)

O God grant that we may always freely acknowledge that whatever has occurred to us is not ours—whether it be talent or inspiration—and that we may never claim as ours what others may have used through us.

♆

BLESSED are the poor in spirit, for theirs is the kingdom of heaven." Yet, it is hard to make poor spiritedness attractive. Still all children of God have told us that humility combined with charity does make a man perfect. Our ordinary excuse for avoiding humility is that as so much of it is sham, and as we are too noble to be insincere, we prefer to be simply proud.

Humility, however, is not making oneself out to be contemptible. It is giving up trying to make anything of oneself. It is, when achieved, not being made out at all. It is becoming invisible to the naked eye. "Do you wish to be invisible?" says the Mahayana scripture. "Then for two years never have a thought of yourself for a single second. After that no one will notice you." Humility's power of being invisible is shown by the actual derivation of the word. It comes from the ground, from the Latin word for the ground, *humus*. Humility is then both invisible and basic, because it is invisible. *The Cloud of Unknowing* makes this clear. The author says that disgust at oneself is merely preliminary humility. We have to begin there, it is true, for we are not ready yet for the real thing and would regard it as the bottomless pit of destruction and not the unyielding ground.

But if we don't get down to the true ground of humbleness our self-disgust can actually become a form of egotism—an absorbed interest in our self-importance if only because of what we take to be our incomparable nuisance value.

This so-called realism can then actually turn into a lie, a fatal form of hypocritical pride. True humility dawns when we are sufficiently purged of the lie of the self for it to be possible for us to begin to have the first faint notion as to what Being, God's Being, may actually be. Then there comes an experience in which the soul knows that it is utterly worthless—so little worth that its annihilation seems not only highly probable but of no significance even to itself.

Beyond that lies the moment when we cannot give even that last remnant of interest to the self. It is lost in an annihilating astonishment at what the Eternal Being reveals Himself to be, once the smoke screen of self is dissipated.

Humility therefore turns out to be in actual fact what the saints have told us that it is. It looks like death but it is really life, and the one way to life. For each time we cast away one of the coats of the self, we are not destroyed, but freed and greatly enlarged. For this is the way to see God, and who so sees Him, is re-created by that sight. No flesh may see Him and live. No creature of self-craving may endure Him who is the denial and destruction of all limitation and separateness.

But the human spirit is of His Spirit, and when it has the courageous love to throw itself away, then daring to lose itself that it may see Him, by that act of humility which abandons all else in itself which is not Him, it is raised to Him. "He has put down the mighty from their seats and has exalted the humble and meek."

ᛘ

(Epiphany)

O GOD who hast taught us that ancient wisdom, when it has become most wise and most prophetic, does seek out and adore the child through whom shall come Thy further revelation: Grant that we, learning from these examples and foreshadowings, may likewise increase in humility, whereby we may grow in that higher knowledge which can discern in the seed the fruit and in voluntary helplessness that new strength which is the power of a new creation.

O God, help us to remember, when the subtle siren note of action calls, that we are nothing, that we can do nothing without Thee.

XIV

PATIENCE

 HIDDEN GODHEAD, THOU ART both the central Force of all things and also their final Purpose. Thou art Thyself before them all, and they all subsist in Thee; and through the fact of Thy existence the world is brought into being and maintained, and Thou art That which all things desire. Give us grace to desire Thee unceasingly and to wait patiently for the consummation of the perfect work of Thy divine Providence.

May we patiently endure Thy absence and vigilantly await Thy coming, so that, when through the constant pain of Thy absence we have become wholly vigilant, we may be comforted with the realization that though we are ignorant Thou art always present.

Grant to us, O God of Patience and Power, the ability to accept with increasing willingness the grace of failure, so that with an entire suppleness of will and promptitude of conduct we may act with freedom from all attachment to what we have mistakenly assumed to be the meaning and purposes of Thy will.

ᛘ

OF ALL the virtues Patience is the least dramatic. Perhaps that is why it is today the least popular. We feel that it is hurry which gets things done. The worse things get, the less we wish to think why; the more we believe we must get a move on. But if we would wait a moment we could not fail to see that the jam we are in is due to our determination to push everything at breakneck speed. Now, however, the concept of growth as being the essence of life, is coming back. Man is master of all the beasts precisely because he takes longer to grow up, to get ready, than any of them; because he takes more time to learn. Man will master himself only when he takes as long to understand himself as he has taken to understand his surroundings. For patience is not just hanging about. Patience is co-operating. We have learned that with Nature. You cannot force natural forces. If you go with them, they will carry you. Thwart them and they will break you. Even in pure thought we have learned the value of patience. From the proved value of second thoughts up to the danger of those premature syntheses which have had equally tragic results in science and theology, we are taught the vital value of the suspended judgment, the danger of the closed mind. Indeed, it is always the sign of a fool, a symptom of oncoming failure, to attempt to force things. Shakespeare's point of view is often pessimistic, but he seems to have concluded that "ripeness is all." Of course Patience is mainly in disrepute because it is thought of as an exasperated, exhausted figure, not "smiling at grief," but telling Destiny to do its worst. True, Patience waits; but it is the quality of the waiting that tells. Beside dull waiting for the next blow, or the impatience which frets and fumes that it is being kept waiting, there is, thirdly, a creative waiting. We must not feel that we are being kept hanging about. As the Gospel says: "In Patience we are to keep our souls." Christ is referring to that earlier counsel, "Wait patiently, *rest* in the Lord, and (in consequence) he shall give thee thy heart's desire." So St. James says further, "Let Patience have her perfect work." For God's work is never hurried, and indeed has in it no element of the climax or the drama because He is an inexhaustible fount of growth, being eternal. We must learn His notion of Time. It is certainly very alien to anything we call up-to-date. Certainly our impatience with Nature, with our fellows, with ourselves, is always spoiling the beauty of design God would otherwise show us every moment. All work has its rhythm: wine, wood, stone, all have their tempo, the time they take to season, to mature. And most of all, our souls. God meant us to have long, patient, beautiful lives, when after each day has been lived fully, without remorse or anxiety, we should come to the full physical ripeness of a glad and healthy death. "Wait upon the Lord, and He shall renew thy strength as an eagle's." If we wait rightly we shall be able to rest; if we rest we shall be renewed and reborn: by patience to work, by sleep to a new day, by death to the life eternal.

ᛘ

AS WE recollect ourselves at this day's ending, O Lord, may we think less of the days which are past or of those which are to come, but with patient concern and contrition be enabled to perceive how far this day we have gone in fleeing from ourselves and how near we have come in our approach toward Thee.

O God grant us the most humble, willing and cheerful patience every time we remember that one day we may know the Truth, one day we may see perfect Beauty, one day we may become capable of selfless love, for one day we may see Thee as Thou art. And grant us an ever-increasing diligence every time we stand in danger of forgetting how few days we have in which to prepare.

XV

HOLINESS

UNITY WHICH ART THE unifying Source of all unity! Essence of all essences! Mind beyond the reach of mind and Word beyond utterance, who alone can give, with true understanding thereof, a revelation of Thyself; we beseech Thee lovingly to reveal Thyself to us by illuminations corresponding to each separate creature's powers, and so draw upwards holy minds into such contemplation, participation and resemblance of Thee as they can attain.

O Holy Spirit who hast awoken in us the hunger for holiness: Grant we beseech Thee, the love and peace which may prepare our hearts to receive the unspeakable gift and joy of total sanctification through Thy possession of our entire souls: Grant, of Thy mercy, that we may, by the longing Thou hast given us, be so wholly emptied of any sense of self that in us nothing but Thyself may be present henceforth and forever.

O God, from whom we have departed so far that though we daily desire Thee more, all we may yet know about Thee is that Thou art utterly above, beyond and different from all that we now know: one thing we still know to ask of Thee: That Thou make us to be utterly above, beyond and different from what we now are.

ᛘ

WHOLE, hale, holy—the three words derive from the same root. By etymology no less than in fact holiness is spiritual health, and health is wholeness, completeness, perfection. God's holiness is the same as His unity; and a man is holy to the extent to which he has become single-minded, one-pointed, perfect as our Father in heaven is perfect.

Because each of us possesses only one body, we tend to believe that we are one being. But in reality our name is Legion. In our unregenerate condition we are divided beings, half-hearted and double-minded, creatures of many moods and multiple personalities. And not only are we divided against our unregenerate selves; we are also incomplete. As well as our multitudinous soul, we possess a spirit that is of like substance with the universal spirit. Potentially (for in his normal condition he does not know who he is) man is much more than the personality he takes himself to be. He cannot achieve his wholeness unless and until he realizes his true nature, discovers and liberates the spirit within his soul and so unites himself with God.

Unholiness arises when we give consent to any rebellion or self-assertion by any part of our being against that totality which it is possible for us to become through union with God. For example, there is the unholiness of indulged sensuality, of unchecked avarice, envy and anger, of the wantonness of pride and worldly ambition. Even the negative sensuality of ill health may constitute unholiness, if the mind be permitted to dwell upon the sufferings of its body more than is absolutely necessary or unavoidable. And on the plane of the intellect there is the imbecile unholiness of distractions and the busy, purposeful unholiness of curiosity about matters concerning which we are powerless to act in any constructive or remedial way.

From our natural state of incompleteness to spiritual health and perfection there is no magically easy short cut. The way to holiness is laborious and long. It lies through vigilance and prayer, through an unresting guard of the heart, the mind, the will and the tongue, and through the one-pointed loving attention to God, which that guard alone makes possible.

ᛘ

O GOD our health, Thou art the Eternal Life who causes and sustains this body: keep it wholly as Thy temple, by making us to live knowing the awful privilege of being the doorkeeper of Thy house: O God our Providence, cause us to make and to give in an equal reciprocation, until we have done with Thy gifts all that was intended and so may yield back the loan gladly to Thee the Lender: O Thou who art our Author, Producer and Critic grant that, freed of self-will, we may do everything always as in Thy presence, by Thy inspiration and for Thy glory.

O Holy One, behind the shimmering multiplicity of outer things may we catch glimpses of Thy unity; beneath the restless activity of the world, Thy creative stillness; above our own wandering thoughts, Thy watchful serenity; beyond our scattered desires, Thy all-embracing love; at the center of our wavering and fragmentary selves, Thy unshakable holiness.

XVI

PEACE

TEACH US TO PRAISE WITH reverent hymns of peace Thy divine peace, which is the source of all mutual attraction; the one perfect Principle and Cause of Universal Peace which broods in undivided Unity upon the World; the Fount of very Peace and of all Peace.

O God who art unknown to us by any name because known to us beyond all definition; closer to us than breathing, nearer to us than we are to our own selves, Thou art within, we are without: Draw us and raise us therefore to that interior height, that we being carried into the darkness of the mind may there abide in that peaceful and imageless knowledge, that interior and total apprehension that Thou hast of all Thy creatures, and they, having this of Thee, become like unto Thee.

ALONG with love and joy, peace is one of the fruits of the spirit. But it is also one of the roots. In other words, peace is a necessary condition of spirituality, no less than an inevitable result of it. In the words of St. Paul, it is peace which keeps the heart and mind in the knowledge and love of God.

Between peace the root and peace the fruit of the spirit there is, however, a profound difference in quality. Peace the root is something we all know and understand, something which, if we choose to make the necessary effort, we can achieve. If we do not achieve it, we shall never make any serious advance in our knowledge and love of God, we shall never catch more than a fleeting glimpse of that other peace which is the fruit of spirituality. Peace the fruit is the peace which passes all understanding; and it passes understanding, because it is the peace of God. Only those who have in some measure become God-like can hope to know this peace in its enduring fullness. Inevitably so. For, in the world of spiritual realities, knowledge is always a function of being; the nature of what we experience is determined by what we ourselves are.

In the early stages of the spiritual life we are concerned almost exclusively with peace the root, and with the moral virtues from which it springs, the vices and weaknesses which check its growth. Interior peace has many enemies. On the moral plane we find, on the one hand, anger, impatience and every kind of violence; and, on the other (for peace is essentially active and creative), every kind of inertia and slothfulness. On the plane of feeling the great enemies of peace are grief, anxiety, fear, all the formidable host of the negative emotions. And on the plane of the intellect we encounter foolish distractions and the wantonness of idle curiosity. The overcoming of these enemies is a most laborious and often painful process, requiring incessant mortification of natural tendencies and all-too-human habits. That is why there is, in this world of ours, so little interior peace among individuals and so little exterior peace between societies. In the words of the *Imitation*: "All men desire peace but few indeed desire those things which make for peace."

ϒ

O MOST Holy Creator, Spirit of Eternal Peace, who brooding upon the primal darkness, brought forth Light: so abide, we beg Thee, with Thy creative peace in our hearts, that we may bring forth the illuminating gifts of Thy presence.

(A Night Prayer)

O God and Father, who givest Thy beloved sleep, Grant us this night and every night, an ever deeper repose, by our bodies resting in Thee, our minds being at peace in Thee, our wills enfolded in Thy will, our hearts enclosed in the measureless content of knowing that because we are able to love Thee Thou hast thereby given us proof and pledge that Thou hast loved us and wilt love us everlastingly.

O God we would not ask for anything but one thing—forgiveness for having made ourselves creatures that are continually craving for self-satisfactions: for the forgiveness that may deliver us from ourselves and grant us release into that selfless peace when at last we may have knowledge of Thy perfect will.

XVII

JOY

THOU WHO ART CALLED THE Transcendent Archetype of Light because Thou fillest every heavenly mind with spiritual light, we pray Thee to drive all ignorance and error from souls where they have gained lodgment, and to give them all a share of holy light, purging their spiritual eyes from the mist of ignorance that surrounds them. Stir and open the eyes which are fast shut and weighed down with darkness, giving them first a moderate illumination, then (when they taste the joy of Thy light and desire it more) giving Thyself in greater measure and shining in more abundance on them "because they have loved much," and ever constraining them according to their powers of looking upward. Let Thy overflowing radiance illumine with its fullness every mind above the world, around it or within it!

O God grant that we may delight in everything only to that degree to which we may see Thee in it, and that whether at the moment it seem to us pleasant or unpleasant may no longer concern us.

O Lord, teach us to know intuitively, constantly, that all is wonderfully, inconceivably well: because Thy constantly instant wisdom and love staunchlessly create those conditions and events in which each soul that Thou hast made may, by the exercise of its full free will, choose Thee and come to Thee, love Thee and rejoice in Thee, be united with Thee and reveal Thee.

♆

PEACE, love, joy—these, according to St. Paul, are the three fruits of the spirit. They correspond very closely to the three essential attributes of God, as summarized in the Indian formula, *sat, chit, ananda,* being, knowledge, bliss. Peace is the manifestation of unified being. Love is the mode of divine knowledge. And bliss, the concomitant of perfection, is the same as joy.

Like peace, joy is not only a fruit of the spirit, but also a root. If we would know God, we must do everything to cultivate that lower equivalent of joy, which it is within our power to feel and to express.

"Sloth" is the ordinary translation of that *acedia*, which ranks among the seven deadly sins of our Western tradition. It is an inadequate translation; for *acedia* is more than sloth; it is also depression and self-pity, it is also that dull world-weariness which causes us, in Dante's words, to be "sad in the sweet air that rejoiceth in the sun." To grieve, to repine, to feel sorry for oneself, to despair—these are manifestations of self-willing and of rebellion against the will of God. And that special and characteristic discouragement we experience on account of the slowness of our spiritual advance—what is it but a symptom of wounded vanity, a tribute paid to our high opinion of our own merits?

To be cheerful when circumstances are depressing, or when we are tempted to indulge in self-pity, is a real mortification—a mortification all the more valuable for being so inconspicuous, so hard to recognize for what it is. Physical austerities, even the mildest of them, can hardly be practiced without attracting other people's attention; and because they thus attract attention, those who practice them are often tempted to feel vain of their self-denial. But such mortifications as refraining from idle talk, from wanton curiosity about things which do not concern us, and above all from depression and self-pity, can be practiced without anybody knowing of them. Being consistently cheerful may cost us a far greater effort than, for example, being consistently temperate; and whereas other people will often admire us for refraining from physical indulgences, they will probably attribute our cheerfulness to good digestion or a native insensibility. From the roots of such secret and unadmired self-denials there springs the tree whose fruits are the peace that passes all understanding, the love of God and of all creatures for God's sake, and the joy of perfection, the bliss of an eternal and timeless consummation.

(A Grace)

CLOSER to us than breathing, nearer than flesh and blood, Grant that this food may be a sacrament between Thee and us, causing us to live more closely with Thee, and ourselves, body, mind and spirit, to become part of that Eternal Life whereby Thy will is done on earth as it is in heaven.

Infinite Godhead, fathomless Ocean of Love, who through excess of joy art ever creating the universe anew; give us grace to go about all our doings cheerfully, rhythmically, with hearts lifted high, knowing that no matter how troubled the surface waters of life seem to be, we are constantly upheld by Thy deep tides of joy.

Grant us vision, O God, that we may see in the content of every moment one more opportunity to turn to Thee with joy—with the joy of quiet confidence, with the joy of a tranquil heart and mind.

XVIII

GRATITUDE

DIVINE RIGHTEOUSNESS WE thank Thee with grateful hearts that Thou art the Salvation and Redemption of all, both because Thou dost not allow things which truly exist to fall away into nothingness, and also because, should anything stumble into error or disorder (and suffer a diminution of the perfection of its proper virtues) Thou dost redeem even this thing from the weakness and the loss it suffers; filling up that which it lacks and supporting its feebleness with Fatherly Love; raising it from its evil state, or rather setting it firmly in its right state; ordering and arraying its disorder and disarray; making it perfect and releasing it from all its defects.

O God, of Thy mercy, crown all Thy goodness to us, by granting to us the joyful virtue of constant gratitude and continual thankfulness: Daily enlarge our capacity for that eternal joy, until we can gladly and from a full heart praise Thee for all Thou doest, because, and only because, it leads us to Thee: Deliver us from any complaining or unthankfulness by showing us that unthankfulness is the refusal to accept Thy purposes, the denial of Thy providence, and gratitude is the joyful acceptance of Thy will, the act of faith whereby, even now, we enter into Thy perfection.

O Merciful God, though our belief in Thee is still so weak that we fail to give Thee cheerful thanks for all those tests and trials whereby Thou art preparing us for Thy presence, of Thy pity grant that this our feeble faith may yet grow through our constant remembering to offer Thee whole-hearted thanks and gratitude for all those manifold mercies whereby Thou hast made open and clear the path whereby we may approach to Thee.

♆

"CALL a man an ingrate and, it is confessed, you can call him no worse," said the well-known eighteenth century Christian Apologist, Archdeacon Paley. But we no longer consider ingratitude serious or surprising. Indeed it is taken for granted. It is a natural way of escape from a galling sense of obligation. We say we have been patronized. Our honor requires that we should show contempt or resentment. So our outrageous egotism can persuade us that our double meanness is simple self-respect.

This gross self-ignorance springs from an absurd misconception about our situation. We have assumed that we have a right to everything we can desire. When we fail we call ourselves dispossessed. Every good thing that befalls us we take for granted. Any check in the flow provokes our indignant protest. It is a grotesque and acutely unhappy state of mind. For it is, in fact, greed grown insatiable. We all know that the complaining are wretched. Intolerable to others they are on the shortest way to becoming intolerable to themselves. At heart ingratitude is a deadly form of disbelief. That is why it creates what it expects. For the sake of a self-love that will not face itself, we have to degrade others; we have to call all kindness only patronage, only the wish to domineer. Conversely, Gratitude is a very practical kind of Faith—not "the lively sense of favours to come," but the spontaneous delight that there is so much selfless good will. And that delight produces what it delights in. Kindness does not mean patronage but the reverse. Kindness is the sense that we are all one, of one kind, kith and kin. So, too, charity in its origin was not the word for alms, but for that gracious and winning overflow of good will that delights in others' happiness. Gratitude and charity are aspects of a single thing, sectors of a single circuit. When that current flows the distinction of giver and receiver disappears. We know that he who can give selflessly can take the sting of patronage out of his gift. But we need to remind ourselves that he who can take selflessly—with undaunted gratitude—can take the alloy of selfishness out of a dubious gift.

Gratitude for all the Truth, Beauty and Goodness that offers itself to us has undoubtedly always led to our being able to perceive more. It is those who have delighted in Truth and believed unwaveringly in it, who have found truth making sense of more and more facts that otherwise were incoherent. So also with Beauty. Design and loveliness appear to await everywhere the mind that has the interest-power to perceive them. And so again with Loving-kindness. Seek for it, believe it is there to be found and find that it has been seeking for you. Indeed we can see further—we can see that he who offers gratitude for Truth finds Beauty. And in turn, grateful for that, he finds still further, Love. And, as the hard, intractable fact that would not fit into the first, too-simple "Natural Law," is found to enlarge and enrich that "law," to increase that meaning, so too with Beauty and Goodness. The "ugly" color, the "muddled" design—the ugliness and the muddle are seen as opportunities for interpretation as our insight grows. The disappointment and the pain —these, too, enrich, not frustrate, the whole, when we can accept them, not grudgingly but with gratitude. The gratitude that at first only gave thanks for all the obvious (and superficial) goods, is crowned in the end by the creative insight that can give thanks to a Creator "who has done all things well."

ᛘ

O GOD grant us to see that day as wasted in which we have found no need to call upon Thee for special grace to bear and to use some strain or disappointment, or no urge to special gratitude for some grace of beauty, love or truth bestowed upon us: Grant us to see that the fuller any day proves to be of such opportunities to call upon Thee, of such invitations to turn to Thee, the nearer we are in our approach to that time when we shall never forget Thee, always see Thee in every event and moment, always trust Thee, constantly be aware of Thy sustaining presence and able to delight increasingly in the growing revelation of Thy perfect being.

O God, our hearts and minds are grateful and filled with thanksgiving, when, in the confusion of striving and effort, we can remember that Thy love and Thy mercy are a certain haven, and that beyond the veil Thou art waiting with outstretched arms.

XIX

FORGIVENESS

O THOU WHO ART THE CAUSE and Origin and Being and Life of all creation, be unto us that fall away from Thee a Voice that doth recall us and a Power by which we rise; and to those of us that have stumbled into a corruption of the divine image within us, be a Power of renewal and reform; and be a sacred Grounding to those that feel the shock of unholy assault, and a Security to those that stand; an upward Guidance to those of us that are being drawn unto Thee, and a Principle of Illumination to those that are being enlightened; a Principle of Perfection to those that are being perfected; a Principle of Deity to those that are being deified; and of simplicity to those that are being brought unto simplicity. And of Unity to those that are being brought into unity.

O God who hast caused us to know Thee first as Forgiver: Grant, we beseech Thee, that we becoming ever more constant in our contrition may be enabled to resume ever more closely our most blessed privilege of fellowship with Thee, and thus, by our walk with Thee, to arrive at union with Thee, who embraces all Thy creatures in Thy everlasting compassion.

O God we thank Thee with all our hearts that Thou hast permitted us to know that we may know Thee: Forgive us that, after many years, we know no more. The door of Thy invitation stands open but we have not yet entered. Pardon us, therefore, with a forgiveness which may sting us through compunction to constant striving, so that we may yet in this day of divine opportunity find that which can alone satisfy our nature and which alone can give us that which the world's sorrow demands of us.

Ɏ

FATHER, forgive us our debts as we forgive our debtors. If you do not forgive those who have trespassed against you, neither will your Father forgive you. So we can't get free ourselves, unless we are willing to offer release to someone else. The Gospels make plain this general liability.

By this law there can be no private salvation. The price of my discharge is the cost of paying what could set another at his liberty. Nor is my discharge to be won by the easy way of being generous to someone I have no objection to—someone who may, even, consider me as spontaneously noble, intervening, like a god, to aid a creature who touches my superior compassion. This is the way we often patronize invalids, poor people, and animals. And it fails because it is not the way to be freed from sin, to be liberated from self.

The real way is really hard. We are not just let pick and choose the object of our charity, and the means of our salvation. For surely our deceitful selves would choose that object and those means which, far from reducing egotism, would inflame it. So the object and means are picked and pointed out for us. Forgive precisely those it is hardest to forgive—those who have specifically wronged me. This, the real thing, is so terribly hard, painfully apt, because, as the shrewd proverb says: "It takes two to make a quarrel." "They hated me without cause" is certainly not the judgment of a detached mind or a forgiving heart. I shan't be able to forgive until I can see, and can say that there was something to be said for the other side. I may, perhaps, have been only passively provocative; but that, if I could grant it frankly, would be to allow I had some guilt, some need to be forgiven, and so I must needs forgive. Certainly, as long as I can think of myself as the innocent wronged party, I am only founding a blood feud, though I myself may never strike a blow. For if I really forgave, no one would ever wish to avenge me. The Dhammapada, devoting itself to the problem of self-salvation, concentrating on the individual issue, makes this terribly plain. " 'He wronged me, he robbed me, he beat me,' in those who so think, hatred will never cease." If I feel myself to be wronged, then in point of fact, I am still hating, or making it possible for others to hate.

Forgiveness, then, is loving. We can receive forgiveness only if we love. Just to be mutely patient, won't serve. "Her sins, which were many, are forgiven." Not because she was made a despised outcast, but "because she loved much." For love, and love alone, can make me forget my wrongs. Justice can't. We are forgiven not because we are the injured party, the underdog, but because we understood why we were attacked, and so were able to forgive. That is why Sankara says karma, the things that happen to you, can never release you; you can be released only by knowledge, and knowledge comes through love. This is real forgiveness, because it delivers me from myself. And this progress of forgiveness does not stop when, through love, I have gotten rid of every sense of wrong I ever had. No, it only begins there. For when I am rid of my self-wrongs, then I emerge into, and confront the wrongs done to, and done by, my society, my heredity, my species.

That is why sainthood's every stage is marked by ever-expanding, interacting forgiving and being forgiven. If we would grow spiritually we should look upon that day being lost in which we have failed to forgive, either through indolence or false complacency. For forgiveness, we see, is just the capacity to understand why the other failed to accept the common responsibility, to seize the initiative and be the first to set the current running again. If I am not always forgiving by love, i.e., understanding some failure by seeing our common part in it, then I am ceasing to grow. I have ceased to recover that full stature and range which belongs to my true nature as one of God's children, the peacemakers.

That, however, does not mean that because I forgive I can make the other person be forgiven. I forgive not to absolve, but to be forgiven. So the person I forgive can be forgiven only in the same way. My forgiving is only an invitation. It is not a compulsion and imposition. He must forgive himself, get himself forgiven by forgiving. Failure to realize that double process has led to much disappointment about forgiveness' redemptive love. I forgave and he didn't respond! But why did you expect he would? Were you told he would? Weren't you told that you were to forgive in order that you, a sinner, might be forgiven? I am not a superior dispenser of absolutions, a redeemer of others in spite of themselves. God, and God alone, forgives and redeems others. One must not be surprised that our forgiving—that all the forgiving that penitents have surely offered, hasn't yet saved the world. Anthony, at the height of his sanctity, once asked his Lord, "What of the other souls?" "Anthony," his Lord answered, "I have given you your soul to save. The others are mine." We must offer Him our total repentance. Then, maybe, when we really can feel, not absolvers of all, but guilty with all, God will redeem us all, because at last we know we are all one.

ϒ

GRANT us, O God of pardon and our peace, that we by Thy forgiveness, being freed from all remorse and anxiety in regard to all temporal things, may henceforth contemplate and reflect only those which are eternal.

Father, who hast kept for Thyself the prerogative of giving us, Thy children, the essential goods of daily bread, vitality and spiritual growing-power; but hast so contrived the interweaving of our lives that we may release one another for further growth in grace; grant that with loving recognition of our mutual dependence as parts of Thy wholeness, responsible to one another and to Thee, we may as eagerly forgive as we eagerly desire to be forgiven.

XX

NON-ATTACHMENT

UNTO THY DARKNESS WHICH IS beyond light we pray that we may come, and may attain unto vision through the loss of sight and knowledge; that in ceasing thus to see or to know, we may learn to know That which is beyond all perception and understanding—for this emptying of our faculties is true sight and knowledge.

O God, for the joy of the freedom of seeking Thee only, may we offer to Thee all those things which those who are not continually seeking Thee must hold to as compensations for the loss of not finding Thee, and anodynes for the pain of the fear that Thou art not to be found.

O God, if we think that we know Thee, reveal to us our utter ignorance, if we imagine that we are near to Thee, show us the abyss that separates us from Thee: But, when we are sunken in the realization of our own ignorance and lost in the desolation of our distance from Thee, then of Thy mercy show us that we are sundered from Thee only by the depth of our own self-love.

GANDHI, a few days before his death, was asked by an anxious but much-tied seeker after liberation, "Is there any way without Renunciation?" "There is no way without Renunciation," he replied, and so set one more seal on the witness of every spiritual guide. The spiritual life, the way to freedom, is through a double, reciprocal process. If it is to work it must be a balanced work. Grace must draw me up. But as soon as Grace begins to pull I discover how I am tied. It is then my turn, now that Grace has given me a new and superior purchase, to loose my old ties. First, of course, I loose those which prevent my responding to Grace at all. If I do that and leave specifically bad habits, then Grace draws me still further and will sustain me still further. It is then that I discover that I could obtain far further freedom and immunity from relapse if I would let Grace lift me right out of my old ruts in which my life has so long run. I must loose every adhesion that I find able to be loosed. God does not ask us to do the impossible but He does ask us to do what He has rendered it possible for us to do. And we generally don't. It is a constant reciprocation between what I find myself ready to give and God can continue giving. If I find no more need of His Graces—if I can find no more room in my life for His designs—if I am content with what He has done for me—then He can give me no more, for there is no room for His gift to come into my filled life. When young William Penn asked

George Fox what he should do about wearing his sword at Court, Fox replied, "Wear it as long as Thou canst." Fox was certain that in this soul Grace was taking the place of all dependence on social respect, that the hunger for God was taking the place of all other needs. So he knew that Grace would make the sword drop off. If then we pray much, that is, if we have a constantly recurring, constantly growing longing for God, we shall, we must, discover a constantly lessening attachment to our tastes, goods, prestige. The growth of one interest is always at the atrophy-price of all the others. Attention, when it is total, is, conversely, total unawareness of any distraction, any other interest. So God weans us, gives us natural, heaven-sent opportunities to let our old tacklings drop. If we take them it is as easy as "casting off" when the tide has come in and one's boat is floating free. It is interesting to note how weak and flaccid such holds, such tendrils, fibers and roots often become in prayer or in the company of those to whom the spiritual life is more real than the material: And how, as weeds, thought to be dead, revive in their strength with one shower of rain, the sinewy grip is refastened round our heart after half an hour with the worldly.

Certainly if we are not continually casting off these old holds, as soon as Grace has shown us that we could—the moment we know that we can depend no longer on them but on Grace—we shall make no further progress. Indeed we may well fall back. The fact that so few of us keep our renunciation, our detachment, balanced with our life of prayer accounts for the poor progress we make after beginning with much promise. Prayer and practice advance together and fall off together. Attachment to God, The One, is only possible with detachment from the triple dissipation of addictions, possessions and pretensions —the lusts of the flesh; the avarice, the money-love, of the world; the pride that is the very Devil. Detachment then is the Holy Indifference which François de Sales prized so highly. It might just as well be called Holy Agreeability. When you are in a plane it is indifferent to you whether you are passing over rough or smooth ground, sea or land—the one thing that matters, if you are to travel and not to smash, is that you must pass over the surface underneath you, you must travel over but you must not touch. That is why Augustine Baker says that, without the grace of constant prayer, self-denial can only make a man hard, while without self-denial prayer is a mere vapor and cannot raise the soul.

ϒ

O GOD, though we have loved the world, yet let us not despair of heaven, for one flash of the splendor of Thy eternity and the brightest time is revealed as shadow: Though we have feared the cost of finding Thee yet let us not lose heart and fail to start again upon our search: For, however feebly we have so far sought, we could not have attempted to begin to find Thee, hadst Thou not already set out to find us, and whatever, O Eternal, Thou hast begun, that, of Thy nature, Thou wilt not only continue but assuredly wilt complete.

O God, whose freedom to create, redeem and sanctify is as infinite as Thy love; loosen us from all adhesions to our willful and ignorant selves, from all inner or outer attachments which hold us back or warp us away from a supple surrender to the free movements of Thy Grace.

O God, our only hope, our one desire; may we, with Thy help, cling only to that which leads us on to Thee, and avoid those occasions in thought, word and deed, which hide Thee from us.

XXI

PRAYER

LET US LIFT UP OUR MINDS IN prayer unto the Primal Goodness, that by drawing nearer thereunto we may be initiated into the mystery of those good gifts which are rooted in Its Being. For the Trinity is nigh unto all things, and yet not all things are nigh unto It. So let us call upon It with holy prayers and unspotted minds and with souls prepared for union with God, that we also may be nigh thereto.

O God who because Thou art the Almighty Creator, canst out of any of Thy creatures form instruments for all Thy purposes, if we will but yield ourselves to Thee, Thou alone knowest our helplessness and that we have no power even to will to be nothing, though we know that we are only an illusion, as long as we are apart from Thee. We beg Thee therefore even this power—to desire to be emptied and that Thou of Thy mercy wilt grant that for us and for all Thou shalt be all in all.

O God we do not ask Thee to answer our prayers, only permit us continually to pray. By Thy grace we are permitted to know something of our willful ignorance. Bring us to a sense of Thy presence that we may know our utter dependence on Thy wisdom, Thy power and Thy mercy, and thus grant us to remain in grateful realization of Thy will being done.

ᛘ

PRAYER is not asking for things—not even for the best things— it is going where they are. That is true; but how are we to go? We must begin where we are. Where we are may be so far out that we may have, not even to begin to pray, but to begin to get ready to pray. The prodigal son did not actually pray his father to receive him until he had done something, until he had set out to find his father.

Our prayer life is largely confused, as is the rest of our life, because our notion of how we behave is the clean contrary of how in fact we do. We think we begin by thoughts, which we believe to be quite easy, then we speak, and finally we complete and crown the process by act. The reverse is what actually happens. Action is what we are always doing, for it is the easiest thing for us to do. Words are more difficult. Thought, the controlled power of abstract attention, is supremely difficult. All living creatures ceaselessly act: of those myriads a very few can find any words: of those, again, few, very few can order their thoughts. Prayer is the supreme mental activity of man.

If, then, a man is to achieve it, he must begin by action, go on to speech and so may end in pure thought. The action he can begin with is: so to arrange that he can reserve time in which prayer could begin. "Muddied water," says Lao-tse, "let stand, will become clear." We must act so that we can let ourselves stand and precipitate our mind. Next, in that time in which we bring our disturbances to a standstill, we can begin to smooth our minds with words. Finally we shall find that, our body being quieted by stillness, and our mind by quiet words, we begin to think why we are quiet and what is the quiet meaning in the words. We begin to pray.

And this, the actual way in which our living processes proceed, is not only the right and only way that we may learn to pray, it also explains why prayer is of such supreme importance. With others as with ourselves we have gotten our actual procedure the wrong way around. We think action is what helps them, that words help action, and thought exists simply to help formulate the fullest action. As a matter of fact, if acts speak louder than words, acts are certainly even more easily misunderstood and more ambiguous. Everyone knows how in attempting to explain oneself one usually makes misunderstandings only the worse.

But that means that thought alone matters? How can thought act? Thought is indeed the only direct action. Consciousness is the supreme fact of the universe. The one real act is the act of one consciousness on another. This can be done most indirectly by one person affecting another's physique, and trusting that the person so affected will understand why he is being treated in this way and so alter his state of mind as the agent desires.

Speech is far less indirect. We can actually argue; but even when we are logical we often fail to carry the person we wish to win, for our logic may seem to him unconvincing, or his suspicion of our motives may make him refuse to be convinced. Our thought can and does penetrate directly into his thought.

Then why are our prayers not answered directly? For two sufficient reasons: firstly, we may lay our offer of good will and devotion in another's mind, but we cannot force him to accept it. God Himself will not override the free will He has given to each soul, and so He certainly will not let us violate that liberty. Secondly, the best and purest gift we can bestow on another is certainly not our notion of what would be best for him. God alone knows that. So our best service to another is to ask God to do His will with this other soul, as in ours. As for ourselves, the journey ends in the same place; not in asking for anything, not for the best, but in going where the supreme love and good will is.

Ɏ

O GOD who hast given us a threefold treasure beyond all price: The Truth that we may know Thee: the life of prayer whereby that knowledge may become actual and instant, and the understanding that through this knowledge and process we shall become like unto Thee:

Grant that we carefully avoiding all that would cloud that knowledge or hinder that practice, may, by continual exercise, at last discover that we have been granted that supreme promise, and have, by Thy great mercy and goodness, entered into the joy of Thee our Lord and everlasting Father.

O God when we have no words, take the will for the words: when the will is numbed take the way of life for the will: when the way of life is wayward, then remember how in the past we have called on Thee for Thy help in the days to come, and deliver us now.

XXII

BEAUTY (II)

THOU ALL-BEAUTIFUL AND more than Beautiful, Thou who art eternally, unvaryingly, unchangeably Beautiful, containing in a transcendent manner the originating Beauty of everything that is beautiful; Thou, the Cause of harmony and splendor in all things, the quality of which Thou dost impart severally according to their nature, shine into our dull minds flashing forth upon us like light a ray of Thy creative loveliness.

O God may we see everything as Thy presence revealed to us that we may reflect Thee: may we hear everything as Thy voice, speaking to us that we may reply to Thee: may we feel every contact as Thy touch that we may turn to Thee: That our eyes thus opened, our ears listening, our hand finding Thy hand, we may follow Thee whither Thou wouldst lead us.

O Perfect God: Thou who alone canst give meaning to beauty and beauty to meaning: Thou knowest that it is our desire for our own wills that alone prevents Thy revelation from transforming our lives and our world. Reveal Thyself that the marring shadow of our selfishness may cease to fall upon Thy work.

ᛘ

BEAUTY is so great, and thought upon it so neglected, that we can reflect on it further. We must consider not only what beauty may be in itself, but what effect it may have on us. It is the third of those three aspects of God, into which the white light of His timeless, conditionless Being is broken into the temporal rainbow of truth, goodness and beauty.

Beauty, however, is a blunted word. There is a deeper meaning for us in its synonym, loveliness. God's beauty tells us something about His love, something which we should never learn if we felt about Him only in terms of our love. For the way we love beauty, the way in which we find loveliness in beautiful things, is different and finer than the usual way in which we love one another. We love in order to be loved, to find, as we say, a return. But when we love beauty we do not expect it to love us. We lose ourselves, we are taken out of ourselves, we stand outside ourselves—which is to say, we experience ecstasy. So our love of loveliness, in one way, gives us no return; because return means coming back to the place where one was. And by being taken out of ourselves we have left the place where we were and ceased to be the person—the return-asking person—that we were.

Yet, on the other hand and equally, our love of loveliness has given us more than any self-seeking, return-demanding love could give. For that return-asking human love could only leave us where we were and—worse—rather more what we were. But the love of loveliness while we thought only of that loveliness, though it seems to care nothing for us, and to draw us to a self-annihilating devotion to itself, was, in fact, working for us, enticing us to our true liberation.

This was the only way to win us to our true nature and full being. God, we begin to see, was indeed teaching us, by what seemed to be His inhuman loveliness, His sublime indifference to us and our adoring admiration, how to love, and by giving us that power of selflessness He was with a patient, amazing providence, giving us a gift we should otherwise have lacked even the power to request. By His loveliness, by the steadily growing revelation of what beauty may be, He is drawing us to selfless love, granting us ecstasy, and transforming us—just as we thought we had lost ourselves, and were careless of the loss—into the reflection and image of That which we had selflessly adored—Himself.

ϒ

O GOD who hast revealed Thyself to us not only as Truth but as Beauty, restrain us from that rude and careless haste which disregards the manifold and incessant beauty of this Thy creation, whereby Thou art revealing Thyself to us: Grant us the recollectedness whereby we may look on these manifest and unceasing revelations of the loveliness of Thy nature and so looking upon these reflections of Thee, we may begin to learn what Thy unveiled splendor must be, Thy formless beauty, of which all beauty of form is but shadow.

O God, help us to know Thy beauty—Thy song of truth that we long for and cannot hear because our ears are dulled by shouts of praise—Thy self-banishing love that we hunger for and cannot feel because our hearts are numbed by the freezing wind of desire—the patient grandeur of Thy Being on which we must ultimately gaze, but which we cannot see because our eyes are glazed with visions of power.

XXIII

GRACE (II)

DIVINE LIFE, ALL LIFE AND movement come from Thee who art beyond all life and beyond every principle of all life. Hence have our souls their indestructible quality, and all animals and plants possess their life as a far-off reflection of Thy Life. Great Giver of life, who bestowest upon men in an overflowing wealth of love such angelic life as our composite nature can receive, turn us and call us from our errors to Thyself and change our whole being to Life and Immortality—a divine and supernatural act; supernatural, O God, as being above the visible order of nature, not as being above the Nature of Divine Life; for unto Thy Life no form of life is unnatural or supernatural.

O God who hast inspired us with the thought that Thou art willing to give Thine own nature to them that ask this of Thee, grant unto us we beseech Thee, that we realizing the supreme generosity of this Thy offer casting aside all that would limit our reception of this unique gift and raising our minds from the hope of any lesser beatitude, may obtain this incomparable endowment, which Thou art most willing to give and we most need.

O God of Silence, Thou knowest how often we mistake the prompting of our self-will for Thy voice: Forgive us this presumption and so direct our attention that we may come to be able to detect in the flow of circumstances where lies the way in which Thou wouldst have us go and may be granted the insight to perceive in every event what may be the particular choice that Thou wouldst have us make.

ᛘ

YOU must co-operate with Grace." That is the central advice of the spiritual masters. And therefore they spend much time in teaching us how we may do so. For, because it is the supreme attainment, it is very difficult to achieve. Here, if anywhere, we find that Razor's Edge, on which we have to balance. Not only most people, but most systems of religious training have fallen over one side or the other. Either they have become purely ethical and practical; or they have become purely magical: Either they have said, "These are the rules, and now it is up to you to keep them or be damned": Or they have said, "Here is complete salvation, self-effort is worse than useless, believe and you are saved." Hence many Asiatic thinkers have divided all religions into those "of self-help" and those "of other-help." And hence we may understand how in spite of the vast sums and energy spent on religion by mankind the results have been so mediocre and the reaction against it is now today so strong. For these alternatives are mistaken. There is a way between the horns of the dilemma. And, as a matter of fact, all those who have attained to the highest sanctity, to complete liberation from themselves and complete enlightenment as to God's Will, Nature and Presence, have succeeded in walking this knife-edge, combining the two elements of Grace and self-effort. Firmly believing that it is God that works, they themselves have worked unremittingly at their side of the task—the hard labor of letting Him have room to work in them. "Work out your own salvation, for it is God that works in you," says St. Paul. Of course it is a paradox in logic. But once we realize what it is that God's Grace is striving to do for us, it is really common sense. We are all of us, as long as we can say "I want this," suffering from the great illusion that we are separate beings, suffering from that basic illusion from which all greed, fear and ignorance have grown. Because it is so profound it does not simply affect our wills. It blinds our understanding, our whole outlook, our entire consciousness. We honestly believe we can have no consciousness but our ego-centered, self-consciousness, and that alone is real. But all the saints tell us that God alone is—all multiplicity, all dualism is illusion. He is "The One without a second." Now this is undoubtedly true. But what can we, as we are, do with such a truth. What the saints say we are therefore bound to misunderstand because (as has been said) It takes two to tell the truth, one to speak it and the other to hear it. We hear only in the terms we can understand. So either we repeat, "He is All," and then add, "the world is illusion," so we cannot and need not do anything. Or we add He is both Creator and Destroyer, so we had best use the old means we have always been employing. These sorry results certainly prove that we have taken our information wrongly. The first step to getting things right is to understand what it is that God desires of us. His aim is not to give us better means to fulfil the ends we now think good—the protection and perpetuity of our present selves. His redemptive purpose is to deliver us from ourselves, to give us not merely new wills but a new consciousness, to unite us with His all-embracing consciousness. It is precisely here that we need incessantly to co-operate with Him, with His Grace. For, because of our rooted illusion of selfhood, we are always striving to make His aid serve the very condition it was meant to cure. We may then say—for it cannot be put without paradox—It is God alone that works. For He alone is real. He is working whenever we desire to be free of self. But if we say, "Because I desire it, therefore I am the worker," the work becomes egotistic, no freedom from self but on the contrary, the enlargement of self. On the other hand, if we say, "Because God works therefore I need do nothing," then the ego remains unreduced, impregnable. For I am willing—quite willing—to remain a separate self. I must wish with all my heart to be other, and at the same time I must understand that that wish does not get me a step toward being another. For I cannot understand what being completely other would be. But by that wish, combined with that humble knowledge of my paralyzing ignorance, I do let God work in me to make me what He is—to make me something that anything still calling itself "I" can never wish with creative power because it can never really understand. That is the mystery of Grace. Words can only point to it vaguely. But it is certainly practical. It is something that can be done. Fail to employ this double process of trust and work, grace and co-operation, and we always get either "evil done that good may come" or paralyzing spiritual sloth. Work with this dual method and we do achieve, as alone is possible, that transcendence of the self, that total consciousness which alone is real sanctity, for it is union with God who alone is Real.

ᛘ

O GOD whose Justice is so comprehending that it is perfect Mercy, whose Mercy is so wise that it is perfect Justice, grant us the supreme Grace to trust Thee always and strive only to do Thy will.

Source of all Grace, may we never lose the realization of our entire dependence on Thee, nor ever tire of asking for daily manna from Thy hand, nor fail to turn to Thee for help in sudden need—another's or our own; for without Thee we can do nothing but interfere with Thy all-wise purposes, but with Thee we can share in Thy providential giving, thus becoming not only receivers but conveyers of Thy grace.

XXIV

RESIGNATION

SUPREMELY DIVINE AND Omniscient Framer of Wisdom prevent us from misinterpreting things above us by our own conceits and clinging to the familiar notions of our senses, thus measuring Divine things by our human standards and being led astray by their superficial meaning. But rather let us humbly resign our own notions and desires, advancing through the negation and transcendence of all things toward That Which is beyond all things. For though Thou art All Things in all things, still Thou art Nothing in any, and the divinest knowledge of Thee is received through Unknowing. It is obtained in that communion which transcends the mind, when the mind turning away from all things and leaving even itself behind, is united to Thy dazzling rays, being from them and in them illumined by the unsearchable depth of wisdom.

Almighty God, by whose power all things are sustained; give us that balanced flexibility of spirit which is perfect trust in Thee, that neither fear nor desire may render us unable to resign our wills unreservedly to Thy will at all times.

O Thou who alone art God, in that Thou canst never be sought in vain, least of all when thou canst not be found as we have defined Thee: Grant that we may never ask for anything that Thou wouldst not give us, but, that in every event, we may be permitted to see Thy perfect wisdom and love bringing us to our supreme need and desire, the knowledge of Thee as Thou art—O Thou whom we fail to find because Thou art so far above our highest hopes.

O God by Thy mercy may we endure being what we are and seeing what we are until through this knowledge and Thy grace we may permit Thee to be in us That Thou art.

ᛘ

FATHER Ignatius, what will you do if the pope dissolves the Society of Jesus?" The founder of the Jesuits, who had owned that when he heard his enemy had been made pope, his bones became like water, replied, "One quarter of an hour in orison and it would be all the same."

Orison is interior prayer, interior prayer is waiting on God, waiting on God is becoming wholly aware of God's presence. We stand looking directly at the cloud of the living light. We realize that we are being confronted and sustained, observed and kept conscious by the infinite presence of the one Reality.

Ignatius was one of the most practical of men. He had little use for theory, and was absorbed in action. So he could not afford to deal in uplift, or wishful thinking. He may not have been a saint of loveliness. But no one has ever denied that he knew what he was talking about, at least in regard to himself and what he could get out of himself. He was neither poet nor braggart. It is worth, then, noting his advice carefully. He did not say Laus Deo, Deo Gratia, or even Fiat Voluntas Tua. After a life of appalling discipline, after achieving quite inhuman detachment, he speaks with precision. He was so controlled that his most intimate companions owned that they never knew if he were happy when genial, moved when displaying anger, dejected when he expressed grief. That is the man who owned that he could not instantly command the perfect composure needed to see swept away the life work for which he had endured such discipline. But he did know exactly where and how to obtain that aid, and he did know with equal precision how long he must take to reach it. He knew he was precisely fifteen minutes out from his true, impregnable base, one quarter of an hour from that frontier which none of the accidents of time may ever cross, and we enter eternity, where the timeless, perfect will of God, alone, is done.

The first step to resignation is, then, to know how far we are from it. Ignatius, because he was a hard realist, believed strongly in a daily examen. The purpose of this is not to bewail failure. I ask myself where have I failed to learn how far I am out, I want to know where I was under such pressure that I failed to do what this morning I resolved I would. Frankly reflective people often say, Well, I know I couldn't stand that! But if we look one step further we see that what we can stand, depends precisely on where we are standing. If you should stand on Jupiter you would be rooted to the ground; if on the moon, you could leap lightly thirty feet. There is a place, we are told, somewhere on the way to the moon where our weight—that is, the pull of the earth on us—would be neutral; we should be able to act with no physical attachment. Put that in the language of the mind, the soul, consciousness, and this is the position, the station which François de Sales calls Holy Indifference—or Holy Agreeability. What makes it possible, is that the pull and purchase of God on our souls, our voluntary nearness to Him, has neutralized the pull of the world on us. We are perfectly resigned, we have fully handed over to Him our desires. Hence, at last, we act with perfect consistency, dependability, reasonableness. We can touch and handle and not be caught and swept away—we are detached from all the accidents of time because we are attached to the Eternal—in whose service alone is perfect freedom.

ᛘ

O GOD we do not know Thee but we know we need to: we do not trust Thee but we sometimes try to: we do not love Thee but we often long to: Pardon our willful ignorance: Forgive our cowardly unfaithfulness: Free us from our obsessional self-love: That we may relinquish our Greed, and so trust Thee: Be relieved of our Fear and thus love Thee; and recover from our delusion of selfhood which is our blinding ignorance and thus at last truly know Thee.

Our God, our Father, our All, may we care only to do Thy will from moment to moment, simply for love of Thee, and without thought of Thy gifts.

XXV

SUFFERING

ABSOLUTE DIVINE GOODNESS, teach us to know evil for what it is: a nothingness, a destruction of the true nature of things; for Good cometh from one universal Cause and evil from many partial deficiencies. Defend us, O God, by Thy infinite Goodness, from all tendencies to evil, that we may be delivered from every taint of those truly devilish evils of brutish wrath, blind desire and headstrong fancy.

O God, whose wisdom is so profound that we often doubt it; whose love is so patient that we often fear lest it could be indifference: Grant unto us some measure of Thy divine insight and heavenly forbearance that we becoming truly patient with our circumstances, our fellows and ourselves, may, with cheerful acceptance, go forward on the path of sanctification on which Thou hast set our feet.

O God, who throughout the ages and to every people hast revealed Thyself, according to their desire, their understanding and their need: Grant unto us, in our present darkness, bewilderment and distress, a revelation of Thyself not according to our contrition nor our desire but proportionate to our great and sore need.

RELIGIOUS people used to talk about the mystery of suffering. A secularized world thinks that phrase is defeatist. Suffering is, most people now would say, a physical thing, a morbid state of the body. Science can put it right. Then suffering will end. Of course they allow that there can be mental suffering. But they generally hold that it is either a by-product of some physical derangement, or, if it has any other cause, it springs from people having too little to do and dreaming about fancies which realism and health would dissipate.

When we reflect on this current outlook it does not appear well-founded, for two reasons: first, we do not seem to have reduced the sum of suffering very much although we have tried very hard, because of the rule that increase of sensitiveness always keeps pace with increase of comfort. Secondly, we have discovered that it is not true that wild life is so very healthy and hearty. Disease has been found present in all present-day animals and in all fossils that have been fully studied. Suffering therefore is not unnatural. In nature it is kept down by the suffering animal being soonest killed. Man therefore has increased his suffering, but the root was there from the beginning.

There is, then, a mystery in suffering. There

may, it appears, be something more deeply wrong with the world than the mistakes or misapprehensions each individual makes. Are we then to be discouraged? A mystery does not mean that it is not to be solved. Most mysteries can be lessened by study. What do we mean by suffering? It is clear that we often speak of two kinds and they are very different. We have only one word for them. The Greeks had two. One they called Patheia. We have taken over that word and used it usefully in science. A pathological state is one in which decay and destruction has set in and which, if not arrested, will lead to death. The Stoics, with their "Apathy," did not first aim at analgesia, but at the cure of a pathological state.

But the Greeks recognized another form of suffering, one quite different and polar from patheia. That they called agonia—their word for a wrestling match. They were right in calling both suffering, but they were further right—and here we have lost touch with their clarity—in seeing that though both had this in common, that they were painful, the painfulness really was not the important thing. The vital question was, what did the suffering mean? Why was it being undergone? What could be made of it? To what would it lead?

This, of course, is the conception of there being an end and purpose in life. And of course modern science has disliked that notion, and having nothing to put in its place it has found that the position that Purpose held in early thought, has now to be taken by the pleasure-pain principle: Life having no discoverable purpose, all you can do with it is to make yourself as comfortable as you can. But to do so, even that word "comfort" has to be degraded. It once meant strengthening. But as the modern world can't imagine any end for which more inward strength is needed, it has made what was a means, an end. So comfort now means collapse into an easy chair.

Yes, the Greeks were right. Natural history and human history have proved there are two kinds of suffering. They both hurt, but they point in completely opposite directions, one to life, and the other to death. And we can probe deeper once we have gone so far. We find that the suffering that makes for death, steadily increases. The pathological state spreads until death intervenes. The more you yield the more it takes. Conversely, we see that the suffering that makes for life if it is faced, steadily decreases: first it is disregarded for the joy that is set before it, and finally it is not felt, and at the utmost end it seems banished utterly. General resistance leads to heightened health, and finally to a new quality of life. Pain can be banished, but only by facing it.

The problem of suffering is, then, not to get rid of anything that might hurt, but so to endure, so to take the initiative against the opponent, so to answer the challenge, that suffering is transmuted into energy and creativeness. Even the eighteenth century called a consummate craftsman (as the highest term of praise) a very painful man. And that rugged old thinker and sufferer, Carlyle, gave a classic definition of genius as the infinite capacity for taking pains. Here we see the word "pain," with all dread gone from it, all slackness and pathology burned out of it. For the secret is in the motive, in the acceptance: the pain is not shunned; it is taken. It is the price, the generously given price, for supreme accomplishment. And more, we see that when the pain is accepted as the price of the achievement, the painstaker, by taking on the pain with generous carelessness, is himself freed from all suffering. If we would be realists, that is the picture that natural science gives us of the struggle of life. At the top of that pinnacle it sees man. But it does not see him finished. He alone of all the creatures, is unspent —has in him a store of creative painstakingness. The choice given him is pathology or agonia, decay or birth, collapse or creation. What is not given him is the pleasure-pain principle. He may collapse or be a creator—he may never be a stabilized beast lapped in arrested comfort. By the pain of creation he may deliver a new creation and at the same time deliver himself from all pain. That is the picture modern research now shows us. It is also a picture which gives us some notion of the Mind who set us this great task, and how and why the saints suffered, strove and won.

Ψ

O GOD, All-wise and All-loving, we are concerned for all we love, for all who in our human imperfect way suffer, for all who yet have to find Thee, for all who yet have even to seek for Thee. Thou too art concerned and we thank Thee that Thou hast taught us this, as Thou hast taught us how to begin to love. Teach us continually how to learn to love in Thy divine and perfect way. Let us never forget, in our imperfect human concern, Thy perfect eternal concern, and grant, as Thou so remindest us, that our concern may grow to be as Thine.

O God, who hast awoken us from the stupor of self-love by the sting of compassion in our hearts; cast, we beg, the beam of Thy enlightenment on our minds, that we may be enabled to understand the meaning of suffering and how Thou wouldst have us act so that pain may reveal its purpose for us and for all Thy creatures.

XXVI

GOODNESS

THOU ONLY GOOD, TEACH US concerning the Goodness of Thy all-transcendent Godhead, that It reaches from the highest and most perfect forms unto the lowest, and still is beyond them, ever remaining superior to those above and retaining those below in its embrace, and so creates and vitalizes and maintains and perfects them all. Whatever living creatures cleave the air, or tread the earth, or crawl upon the ground, and those which live buried and covered in the earth; all these are endowed with soul and life because the Good exists. And all plants derive from the Good that life which gives them nourishment and motion. And even whatsoever has no life or soul comes into the estate of being through the Good.

O God, though we are hard and shrunken, we know that we have by Thy will within us the flower of the Life Eternal, may therefore the light of Thy wisdom radiate us; the warmth of Thy love rouse us; the water of Thy peace enrich us; that we may cast the husk of selfhood and rise up before Thee, an abundant harvest of goodness to Thy everlasting glory.

O God grant us the gift to know that we have nothing; the power to feel that we are helpless; the grace to know that we are graceless: that we may rejoice that we are thereby being emptied of self and that we have in this emptying the proof of Thy incoming presence and the promise of Thy fullness.

ᛉ

THE Good, the True, the Beautiful—about the supreme worth of these three things, till lately no one had a doubt. But Beauty is now suspect, for fear it should only be prettiness. And Goodness is in even worse repute. There is no doubt of this. People are ashamed to be thought good. The common assumption seems to be that goodness, if you psychoanalyze it and so find out the truth about it, is either hypocrisy or a timid shrinking from life.

Sometimes it helps to take a word's opposite if we would understand its positive meaning. The reverse of goodness is badness. When we say a thing is going bad we mean that it is becoming corrupt: when we say—as of food—that it is still good we mean that it is still in the state in which it will nourish life. The French word for good links with the Scotch word "bonny," a word of health. So, as Good is thus linked with Hale, and Hale, as we have seen, is linked with Holiness, total goodness, completed goodness is Perfection.

If, then, we consider goodness in its deepest sense we shall find that it is a growth word, a word for that dynamic reaction which is the basic evidence of Life's presence. In this world every living thing has always to be making good—or it will go bad, putrify. There is no rest for any form of life. "He that is not getting better is getting worse"—the grim Stoic motto found written in Oliver Cromwell's Bible, states the case. The main trouble about goodness springs from the fact that those who are active generally disregard the fact that they have to grow. They therefore try to alter things by violence in the belief that changed circumstances make changed men. On the other hand, just abstaining from violence is not enough. He who would, with God's Grace, grow into a new person with new apt force, must work harder than any go-getter. Goodness is then the first step and not the least difficult in self-transmutation. We shall not achieve it unless we know what we are about. William Law, the Anglican spiritual master, when criticized for advocating saintliness replied that if we aimed at perfection we might attain goodness. He saw that the spiritual life is a growth and goodness should not be blamed or despised because it is not perfect—do you gather fruit from buds? We shall, however, never attain to wholeness, fruition, total knowledge and power unless we are prepared first to strive simply to be good.

There is more than a little truth in the old statement, A man will never be a saint unless he can first prove himself a gentleman. Conversely we shall never be prepared to work hard at fulfilling what have been called "the eternal commonplaces of goodness" unless we understand that these are the beginner's exercises, the child's stumbling efforts to walk, that preceded, and must precede, the expert's masterly execution, the athlete's record-breaking. We practice goodness, must practice it and alone can have the patience to practice it, because we know that the good is only a first step. It is true that unless goodness is a step to holiness then the French saying is correct—the good is the worst enemy of the best. Goodness is then to be striven for as a means, not as an end. The goal for which we strive and for which everything is to be won and then offered is Perfection —"Be ye Perfect as your Father in Heaven is Perfect."

Ψ

O GOD, of Thy mercy may we know Thee sufficiently to love Thee so much that we may be able to bear knowing ourselves sufficiently to dare to love ourselves no more.

Since every good gift comes from Thee, our Father, we Thy children stand here empty before Thee, asking only to be filled with thoughts of Thy goodness, that our hearts may overflow in silent adoration.

XXVII

PERSISTENCE

GRANT US GRACE TO LOVE THEE in full measure and to persevere in our search for Thee, since Thou, the Creator of all things, Thyself lovingly yearneth after all things, perfecting all things, conserving all things, attracting all things back unto Thyself through nothing but excess of Goodness. For the yearning Love which createth all the goodness of the world being pre-existent abundantly in Thee, the Good Creator, allowed Thee not to remain unfruitful in Thyself, but moved Thee to exert the abundance of Thy powers in the production of the universe.

O Thou who hast given us desire without knowledge, devotion without understanding, faith without sight: Grant us unwavering Persistence, that we following faithfully in the steps of Thy commandments, may come to that hour of illumination when we shall know even as we are known.

O Eternal Father, Most Holy Spirit, who in Thy wisdom has created this universe in a marvelous series of ascending steps whereby all Thy creatures may rise to Thee: Grant that, as Thou hast permitted us to discern the visible stages whereby Thou hast brought us to our present station, we may now come to perceive that vast invisible series that rises from this our present degree to Thy sublime supremacy; so that we, shunning all purblind complacency, may set ourselves steadfastly toward that tremendous ascent, and, with our vision longing for the invisible, looking upon this life as but an entrance, with constant gratitude that Thou hast permitted us to conceive of Thee as our goal, we may unwaveringly press on to the prize of our high calling.

ᛘ

SOME saints have said that no virtue is greater than Persistence. Certainly no one can have watched the spiritual life in himself or in others, without seeing that lack of this virtue accounts for most casualties. No doubt carelessness in using other graces is a predisposing cause of such disaster. But on the death certificate of most souls, the reason for decease must be put down to heart failure. Indeed the whole spiritual life is a series of endurance tests. St. Benedict, building his enduring system, warns us against "the zeal of novices." St. Philip Neri, devoted as he was to the young, said he put little trust in fledglings that thought, because they could flutter, they could fly. So often the religious life begins surprisingly well. But whether emotionally satisfying or intellectually exciting, neither of these pleasant states is going to last. The world has two explanations for that: First, we are told that religious teachers don't know their business. If they did, there would be a standard textbook for Sanctity without Strain. The second explanation closes the matter: The difficulty of the religious life shows that the whole thing is "unnatural." It is a search for an illusion. The disappointment is a warning to go back to a life of sane ease and "average sensuality." But is there an art that can be achieved without great effort? Further, does not the learning of any art, any technique show the same unpleasant rhythm? Early interest and "beginner's proficiency" always turn into the steady student's drudgery and his relapses into baffling incompetence. The same is true of sports also. Anyone wanting to master any skill has to learn that there is an optimum pace at which he must go if he would stay the journey. If you push on at top speed, you will tire and stale long before the end. Mountain guides start out at what seems to the impatient novice an exasperating dawdle. They might be taking a casual stroll—not out to conquer a peak. But they know the pace that can be kept up, and may need to be kept up on a cliffside, in a blizzard and when the high air is so rarefied that the lungs labor as though suffocating.

How then are we to gain this essential Persistence? We must banish from our minds the thought of quick, showy results. And yet we must be unremittingly industrious. We must be patient when the tide is out and yet never lose vigilance, so that the moment the tide turns we take it. That can only be done if we have Right Knowledge, if we know clearly what it is that we have set ourselves to do. Few things frustrate religion more nowadays than the general mistake as to religion's end and aim. When it is approved at all, it is approved as a therapy. When it begins by working like a therapy and health cure we are certain that we have found its meaning. We feel sure that it is *this* that the saints—under all their awkward, "spiritistic" verbiage—were achieving, whether they knew it or not. So when religion fails to make us feel any longer good, we drop it. But if religion's aim—as it has always claimed—is to produce in us a complete change of consciousness, to bring us through the death of our ego into another "world," then we should not be surprised that the process is both painful and lengthy. The greater the goal the more we are prepared to endure for it. We fail in persistence because we are ignorant of the prize. But how can we know about that? There is only one way to learn about the splendor of any art. There is only one way whereby we may ever gain the courage to go on climbing the "strait and narrow way." There is only one way to know that a thing is so worth doing that it is worth doing—and for a very long time—badly, very badly. That only way is by being with those who have long been on the way. No art is to be learned, no student but will remain a bungler, unless he work with a master or see the work of masters. These masters tell us, and prove it by their lives and work, that however hard Persistence may be, it is essential; however painful, it is invincible. "The Devil's chief weapon is discouragement": the unpierceable armor against that weapon is Persistence.

Ψ

O GOD, when because of interruptions we cannot recollect ourselves and persist in our waiting so that we may come into Thy presence, of Thy mercy, let the sense of our loss and bafflement admit Thee to some depth of our being, some level of our will. For even when we are least disturbed and most attentive still art Thou infinitely far from us by any effort that we may make to approach Thee; still art Thou unattainable by any power of attention that we may command. All our hope of drawing nearer to Thee depends wholly on our sense of helpless absence, that this, appealing to Thy compassion, may draw Thee to approach us and turn us toward Thee. For only by the mystery of Thy condescension, and by no effort of our will, nor systematic skill of our mind, nor grasp of our intellect, may we be brought in any wise nearer to Thee. Our intensest concentration may not pierce into Thy plenitude, any more than our most wayward thought may apprehend Thy intensity.

(A Morning Prayer)

O God teach us to know that by Thy mercy we are again at the beginning of another day and that this day is not the mechanical repetition of those that have passed and been by us forgotten. By Thy grace this day has never been before and by Thy justice will never come again. During it, whatever else may happen, grant us that we may persist in that one thing that matters, adhering to Thee, so that at its close we may be farther from ourselves and nearer to that Goal in which alone we may find the purpose of our life and the lasting rest of our soul.

XXVIII

DEATH

IMAGELESS AND SUPERNATURAL Simplicity, teach us in this life how to seek Thy divine enlightenments through that sacred veil which enwrappeth spiritual truths in terms drawn from the world of sense and from a variety of separable symbols, so that hereafter when we are incorruptible and immortal with our mind made passionless and spiritual, we may participate in a spiritual illumination from Thee, and in a union transcending our mental faculties, may amid the radiant splendor of Thy dazzling rays, in a diviner manner than at present, be like unto the heavenly Intelligences.

O Father of Lights, dwelling in splendor unapproachable, unsustainable by our clouded and shrunken senses: grant to those from whom Thou hast lifted the veil of the flesh, that, drawn and sustained by Thy love, they may henceforward go unrestrained toward Thee, until they come into the glory of Thy presence, and, seeing Thee face to face, are transformed into Thy blessedness.

O Invisible God, who knowest how we are beguiled by this visible world, grant that we may become increasingly aware of those presences whereby Thou hast caused us to be encompassed both for our succor and as an abiding witness of all our actions, that we may constantly live as those who know that they shall give an account for even their most hidden deeds.

ᛘ

HE MAY not truly know how to live who has not first learned how to die." That common medieval aphorism seems to us both morbid and absurd. How can you learn to die? Unfortunately that Accident of accidents will no doubt one day befall me—unless rejuvenation is discovered in time. But meanwhile it is possible by distraction most days "to enjoy an indefinite reprieve." Nevertheless this matter of Death is one of the cardinal points on which religion and science agree. Death is not only as natural as birth: it is as necessary to the processes of Nature. A life process that had birth without death would soon abolish itself. Death sweeps Life's path, trims Life's lamp, lifts the husk from life's flower. And, individually, every person first "evolves" and then "involves," "inliminates" and then "eliminates." Death and disease are not the same thing. There need not be disease. But there must be and should be death. That means that there can be a healthy death. And that seems to us a paradox—indeed a heartless jest. Yet why do we refuse to examine the statement? We refuse to accept it because we say that it is too good to be true. Even if death is anaesthetic, it is the utter and horrible frustration for there is nothing beyond, of course. And we so dismiss the post-mortem life because, since we ceased really to want to know about it, we have given all our attention to this bodily life, to the vain effort to fix and set this life. So we left the life after death to the fairy-tale tellers. But death and what follows, life-and-death as a single cycle is neither fairy tale nor joke. So death is, as we should expect, just as serious, meaningful and effortful as birth. It is not poetry but fact that death is a birth. For this life is just as much an embryonic experience as was our life in the womb. An embryo might well think that its womb life was all—any postnatal life must be under such utterly different conditions as to be ridiculously inconceivable. Yet not only is such a life ahead of it and that life completes its present life, but its present life, every hour of it, decides what its afterbirth life will be—the life of a healthy person, a cripple, an imbecile, a monster. So with us and Death. The belief in "survival," is no fairy tale, no joke: it is serious, dead serious. "As a man sows so shall he reap" is only cheering to those who have sown well, right up to the last moment. All the religions that have known about spiritual things have then stressed not only the importance of every hour you lived but also of the very hour of death. That, we said, is a further proof of the absurdity of all these fancies. It was not. For all these religions, because they believed in death and the afterlife, believed in the enormous value of having been born, of being able to live here in a human body. For while so living, so sheltered, we can learn to know ourselves and to direct our minds and wills. Death does not imprison. It sets us terribly free—to go on swiftly to God our Goal, if we have learned to align ourselves while we were in this "gun-barrel of the body"—to go to pieces, if we have not.

ᛘ

O INVISIBLE God, Father of all spirits, who hast taught us that love is stronger than death: Grant unto us, by Thy wisdom which can forget nothing; by Thy love which embraces everyone; by Thy power which sustains all: that we may always remember with hope and love in Thee all those who have passed out of our sight and that by our realizing our communion with them in Thee, we may be permitted to aid those who still in Thy purposes need our compassion and we ourselves be aided by those who from their present station nearer to Thee feel Thy compassion for us: Grant this, O Father, who of Thy loving instruction of us doth mediate Thy mercies to us through those whom in Thee we have loved and love.

Lord of life and death and more abundant Life, who hast set a door of birth leading from one into another; help us to keep our focus clear and sharp during this earthly span, distinguishing the real from the unreal, shadow from substance, so that entering into Life Eternal our souls may be fully awake to the wonders that lie ahead.

XXIX

MORTIFICATION

WELLSPRING OF ALL WISDOM, LET us be transported wholly out of ourselves and given unto Thee! For it is better to belong unto Thee and not unto ourselves, since only thus can Thy divine giving be received, if our wills are one with Thine.

O living God, teach us to die daily and hourly to everything that does not bring us nearer to Thee; until by Thy grace we may finally strip off the last vestiges of our clogging shadow-selves and dwell forever in the light of Thy presence, which is Life Eternal.

ᛘ

MORTIFICATION is as unpopular in most forms of modern religion as sanctity is rare. Salvation, it is repeatedly said, is to be found by "entering into the joy of the Lord," not by grimness and self-regarding asceticism. By itself this statement is undoubtedly true. However, the corollary which would hold that therefore in morally indifferent matters a religious person can act in the manner designed to afford himself the maximum pleasure and the minimum pain and effort, is just as surely false.

Theology teaches that in our natural unregenerate state we are fallen creatures, that we have separated ourselves from God, forgotten who we are. Our salvation, the purpose of our existence, consists in becoming reunited to God, in recollecting our true existence. This redemption is achieved, in so far as we have power over it, through the twofold process of mortification and prayer. To overcome our habitual greed, to ignore our ingrown fears, are laborious and often painful procedures. Anyone, however, who consistently shirks this labor and shuns this pain can know but little of God.

Although, for the sake of classification, the spiritual life can be divided into prayer and mortification, in fact the two are organically related. They are not separate things to be practiced apart from each other. Jeanne de Chantal says that it is dangerous to pray without constant mortification: for most of us it is not dangerous but impossible. The will that habitually grants all that the sensual and egotistical appetites desire, can never be sufficiently recollected to attend for long to that pure love and understanding which is the antithesis of craving and selfishness.

True mortification consists then simply in preferring God's will to one's own. The only test whether an act is one of mortification or springs from self-indulgence is whether it increases our love of God and our neighbor. To be entirely free from desire for anything but God's will is the state of the saint, one who is fully enlightened. To strive to prevent anything but God's will from commanding ours is the necessary preparation for sanctity. When we have passed through complete self-denial we enter eternal infinite joy. It is eternal and infinite, for it is not ours but the joy of God.

♆

O GOD, who hast taught us that death is the Gate of Life; teach us that, by dying daily to ourselves, through true unselfishness toward our fellows and true devotion to Thy will, we may already, in this mortal life, be enabled to enter Thy eternal life and so be peacefully prepared to find, when Thou shalt grant it, in death that full and final release from the last fetter of self-will.

Grant us the wish and will to leave the chains of craving that bind us and keep us from Thee, O God; grant us the strength to cast them off and come to Thee.

XXX

TIME

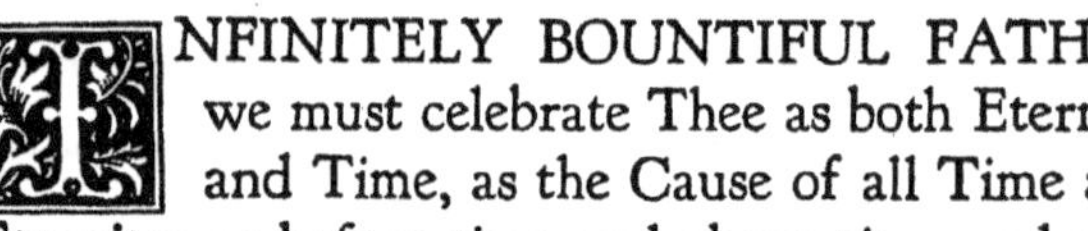

NFINITELY BOUNTIFUL FATHER we must celebrate Thee as both Eternity and Time, as the Cause of all Time and Eternity; as before time and above time and producing all the variety of times and seasons; and again, as existing before eternal ages, in that Thou art before eternity and above eternity, and Thy Kingdom is the Kingdom of all the eternal ages. Teach us to know Eternity as the home of things that are in being and Time as the home of things that are in birth.

Father, Thou that art the Eternal, whom therefore the Past and the Future obey, so keep us as Thy children, by constant contrition free of all regret and remorse and by constant adherence from all anxiety and foreboding, that we thus being enabled to know that all Time is in Thy hand may be brought to that blessed peace, joy and liberty of Thy ever-creative presence.

O God unknown and yet well-known, the distant and inconceivable goal of all our journeying, the instant presence at every step, Grant that we knowing Thee increasingly as our strength, our wisdom and our love, may, when the veil is lifted and we see Thee as Thou art, know that it is Thou and no other who hast been the constant companion, sustainer and guide of all our pilgrimage.

ᛘ

IT IS strange that in our religious life we Westerners have given so little real attention to Time. "Time," we say "haunts modern man." Sociologists tell us that we are more time-conscious than any other generation. The medievals were content when, on their sun dials, they split the hour into quarters. Then came clocks with minutes and trains, timed to the minute. After that we had seconds to count our fevered pulses. And then split seconds to time our racing cars. And, strange to say, in our religious life our attitude toward Time has been as hectic. In the eighteenth century Instantaneous Conversion became the one technique among Protestants for producing "metanoia," change of character and consciousness. Since then we haven't produced any other method. On the contrary, we have thrown ourselves into holy hustles to sell the world a vision we ourselves have never had time to take in. Yet Time must be understood and its rules learned if we would use our lives as they were meant to be used—to find God. The right attitude to Time is hard to keep—it is a knife-edge. Generally men have fallen off on the one side or the other: Either they have treated Time as an illusion and sat down to wait for Eternity. Or Eternity was dismissed as the great fraud and men rushed headlong to catch Time and turn it into everlastingness. Both were mistakes. For Time is the only way to Eternity. But to go that way we must go at the Right Time, the right pace. And we can add a word more to the medieval advice "Don't rush." Some of the Sanskrit teachers give valuable time tables for those who have decided that they wish to spend their lives on the path to God. They do not question His Grace—that He can come to us in a moment. But they say we must co-operate with His Grace. And they point out that this co-operation, our making up our minds wholly to ask Him to alter them wholly, takes time. He is patient. As much as we ask, He gives—and indeed always more. But He cannot give what we still don't wish, and so could only misuse. It takes us years to make up our minds, to know what we really want, to pull ourselves together. Twelve years, they say, is common time that we spend before we can bring ourselves to ask with our whole hearts, and so He can give, as He would and will, in a moment all He wishes.

Let us then plan with this precious supply of Time that He has given us: lay it out steadily: a Twelve Year Plan: that month by month we may win that power over our entire selves that at last permits us to offer ourselves to God wholly and for good.

ᛘ

O GOD who in Thy mercy hast forgiven us the Past, grant therefore that we may leave it for good with Thee to whom alone it now belongs: Thou in Thy wisdom hast not given us the Future: grant therefore that we may leave this also with Thee in whom alone it exists: Thou hast in Thy grace, given us the Present where now and only we may meet Thee: Grant us therefore that we may not absent ourselves from Thee by vain regrets and vainer apprehensions, but presenting ourselves wholly before Thee in constant readiness, accept from Thee this supreme gift, beg of Thee to inform us how Thou wouldst have us deal with it and grant us the strength to perform this Thy instant purpose according to Thy holy will.

O God in whose eternal wisdom alone is comprehended the mystery of Time, we thank Thee for the Past because Thou hast forgiven it: we thank Thee for the Future because Thou hast hidden it: we thank Thee for the Present because Thou art wholly Present in it, to meet us with Thy creative, redemptive and sanctifying power, if we will awake from all dreams of past and future to live in this Thy instant reality.

(On Parting)

O God with whom there is neither distance nor time, when we are scattered by distance and hurried by time bring us back through the recollection that as soon as we will be still we may know that Thou art always present with us and with Thee in that present are all those, wherever and whensoever they be, who love Thee and whom, in Thee, we love.

XXXI

ETERNITY

 FOUNT OF PERFECTION! THOU art the Form producing form in the formless, as a Fount of every form; Thou art Formless in the forms as being beyond all form. Thou art the Being that pervades all beings at once though not affected by them. Thou art Super-Essential as transcending every being. Thou settest all bounds of authority and order; yet Thou hast Thy seal beyond all authority and order. Thou art the Measure of the universe. Thou art Eternity and above Eternity and before Eternity. Thou art Abundance in those beings that lack, and a Super-Abundance in those that abound; unutterable, ineffable!

O God the King of Glory who hast given us the glorious hope of the Life Eternal; Grant that we, growing in that hope, may so advance in that faith which can remove mountains and that charity which calleth nothing its own, until, grounded in faith, hope and charity we shall know that neither life nor death, nor height nor depth nor any other state or condition shall any longer separate us from Thee, Thou that art our strength and our salvation and our exceeding great reward.

O God, we praise before Thee the glorious company of Thy saints, who, though men of like passions with ourselves, were raised through their desire to partake of Thy nature, so that they have become the channels of Thy grace. Grant, that as they have entered on Thy eternal life we may now have communion with them in Thee, and, by the series of their examples and the number of their virtues, may rise through this ladder of perfection, until we with them may behold Thee face to face.

†

WE HAVE had as much trouble with Eternity as with Time. Even when we call God The Eternal, we seldom reflect why that term is so often used by the saints when they speak of Him. We still think that it only means that He is Everlasting, The Ancient of Days. That makes Him as distant from us in Time, as, when we think of Him as big, He is made distant from us in Space. Yet we know that His Transcendence and His Immanence are not two separate things. They are only two phrases in which we try to think simultaneously that He is beyond all smallness and bigness, still closer than any intimacy however exclusive; still vaster than any dimension however supreme. So too with His relation to Time. God is not so Ancient that He sees us—if at all—as far less than instantaneous flickers.

He alone is really and fully present in any and every event. Not only is His Eternity not infinitely extended Time. Time is His manifestation of His Eternity, His terrific Immediacy, mediated, serialized to us, so that we may sustain what otherwise would be for us an intolerable intensity of Presence.

So, day by day, God is, through Time, assembling us, drawing us, pulling us together, giving us, if we would do His Will and seek His Light, a presence of mind, an awareness of instant complete significance, a liberating sense of immediate, total meaning. Our lives are nothing but futility unless they are a preparation for Eternity. For, every day if we will, we can assemble ourselves out of the dissipation of irrelevance into an evermore complete co-ordination. Finally, we may stand in and sustain the total Timeless intensity. We shall have gathered up all our times into one act of grateful acceptance, thankful recognition: we shall have become single-hearted instantly and forever: we shall have the Beatific Vision seeing God, the Eternal.

ᛘ

O ETERNAL Reality, shrouded in light, let Thy holy fire of love burn through all barriers, that our prayer may move steadily inward beyond ourselves toward Thee, O timeless and spaceless Being.

O Thou who inhabitest Eternity, and dost know that the discursive thought of man cannot reach that instant intensity, nor the imagination of man that boundless transparency; we pray Thee of Thy mercy to deepen and expand the longing heart, that it may, like a quiet lake before dawn, reflect in purity the coming Light.

ASPIRATION

Epilogue

ST. ANSELM: FROM *PROSLOGIUM*
Abridged

ORD, TEACH ME TO SEEK THEE and reveal thyself to me when I seek thee, for I cannot seek thee except thou teach me, nor find thee except thou reveal thyself. Let me seek thee in longing, let me long for thee in seeking; let me find thee in love and love thee in finding. Lord, I acknowledge and I thank thee that thou has created me in this thine image in order that I may be mindful of thee, may conceive of thee and love thee; but that image has been so consumed and wasted away by vices and obscured by the smoke of wrong doing that it cannot achieve that for which it was made except thou renew it and create it anew.

Is the eye of the soul darkened by its infirmity, or dazzled by thy glory? Surely it is both darkened in itself and dazzled by thee. O Lord, this is the unapproachable light in which thou dwellest; for truly there is nothing else which can penetrate this light, that it may see thee there. Truly, I see it not, because it is too bright for me. And yet, whatever I see, I see through it, as the weak eye sees what it sees through the light of the sun, which in the sun itself it cannot look upon.

O Supreme and Unapproachable Light! O Whole and Blessed Truth, how far art thou from me, who am so near to thee! How far art thou removed from my vision, though I am so near to thine! Everywhere thou art wholly present, and I see thee not. In thee I move, and in thee I have my being, and cannot come to thee; thou art within me, and about me, and I feel thee not.

Trinity which exceedest all Being, Deity and Goodness! Thou who dost instruct us in Thy heavenly wisdom! Guide us to those mystic heights which exceed light and more than exceed knowledge, where the simple, absolute and unchangeable mysteries of heavenly Truth lie hidden in the dazzling obscurity of the Secret Silence, outshining all brilliance with the intensity of their darkness, and surcharging our blinded intellects with the utterly impalpable and invisible fairness of glories which exceed all beauty! Such be our prayer.

HYMN

O Thou, Who art where words must cease
Where thought can only bar,
Thy still Eternity is peace
Time-fevered as we are.

O Infinite, none can contain,
No smallness may exclude,
When past the self's extent we gain
Thy spaceless plenitude.

All Beauty that can raise the soul
To self-less ecstasy,
Is but a fragment of that Whole
Which still but shadows Thee.

All Truth that any man has heard,
In Law, Equation, Verse,
Is a faint echo of Thy Word,
Uttering the Universe.

All Love Humanity may name,
Love that annihilates wrath—
A slag, left by the all-fusing Flame
That is Thy Giving-forth.

We worship Thee within the mind
And in the selfless heart
Not only as the Wise and Kind,
But, simply, Thou That Art

From highest Heaven our eyes we raise,
They only pause a while—
The child turns from his birthday gift
To his dear Father's smile.

So when the praise of Heaven would
Be task beyond our skill,
We say, Thou art the Fatherhood,
And we are by Thy Will.

So when the praise of Heaven sounds
A term beyond our thought,
We say, Thy Being has no bounds,
And in Thee we are nought.

Exiled, in Chains, Entombed,
Deliver me from me.
Freedom may only be resumed,
Annihilate in Thee.

Distraction from Thee is a grief,
Pleasure benumbs the heart,
That, in Death will break with the relief
Of knowing That Thou Art.

We know Thee not. Thou knowest us,
Not as ourselves we know.
Thou knowest selves we have forgot,
And selves to which we go.

Thou comest not, Thou goest not,
Thou wert not, wilt not be,
Through all our years we have but sought
Thy Perfect Instancy;

Yet every breath has nearly caught
Thy awful Constancy.

Thou Art, O Presence so enwrought
All else is nullity.